HAWKING AND FALCONRY
FOR BEGINNERS

This book is dedicated
to the memory of my father, William Hallgarth,
a man who realised the value of patience
and the rewards of common sense.

One book, delivered as promised, Dad.

The author with his favourite Harris, Vixen, and his favourite pointer, Stan.

HAWKING AND FALCONRY FOR BEGINNERS

An introductory guide to falconry
and training your first bird

A.J. HALLGARTH

hancock

house

ISBN 0-88839-549-3
Copyright © 2004 A.J. Hallgarth

Cataloging in Publication Data

Hallgarth, A.J. (Adrian John), 1968–
    Hawking and falconry for beginners : an introductory guide to falconry and training your first bird / A.J. Hallgarth.

Includes bibliographical references and index.
ISBN 0-88839-549-3

    1. Falconry. I.Title.
SK321.H24 2004   799.2'32   C2004-903873-7

Printed in Korea: PACOM
Editor: Margaret Jetelina
Cover Design: Rick Groenheyde
Production: Margaret Jetelina, Ingrid Luters
All photographs © ***Niall Benvie*** unless otherwise credited.
www.nialbenvie.com
Front cover photograph: A freshly equipped young hawk on the fist.
Back cover photographs: *(Top)* A young male Harris hawk attacking a lure.
                        (Bottom) The hood seating is put into place on the head.

Published simultaneously in Canada and the United States by

HANCOCK HOUSE PUBLISHERS LTD.
19313 Zero Avenue, Surrey, B.C. V3S 9R9
(604) 538-1114 Fax (604) 538-2262

HANCOCK HOUSE PUBLISHERS
1431 Harrison Avenue, Blaine, WA 98230-5005
(604) 538-1114 Fax (604) 538-2262
Web site: www.hancockhouse.com *Email:* sales@hancockhouse.com

Preface

At eight years old, I was, as is known today, a "Latch Key Kid," returning each day from school to an empty house in an industrial city in the north of England. You see, when I was four years old, my parents split up, and I found myself in the sole care of my father, who, love me dearly as he did, still had to bring home the bacon; he was as an industrial chemist for British Steel, a job which required him to work long hours. So I was passed from one childminder to another until I was old enough to stay at home by myself, at which point I took a great interest in reading. One day, while foraging through a section of the local library, I came across a book by author Barry Hines called *A Kestrel for a Knave*.

My decision to read this book was based solely on the cover, which depicted a small boy holding a bird of prey on his fist. Once started, it took me just six hours to read the book from cover to cover (no mean feat for an eight-year-old!), and this started what was to become my lifelong obsession with birds of prey.

For those of you who haven't read Hines' book, it details the story of a young boy growing up in an industrial northern town in England, not too far from where I lived, who experienced many of things I was going through at that time. He sought the escape and company of a kestrel, which was taken as a young bird from its nest. The boy eventually managed to train the bird using the techniques I now know as falconry.

It was beyond my comprehension that anyone would be able to not only tame, but also fly free one of these awe-inspiring creatures, and have it return. So the next day I returned to the library and looked up any title I could find relating to the sport of falconry. I found two books, *A Garden of Eagles*, by David Fox, and another book whose title I cannot remember, but whose photographs and text I will never forget. One particularly memorable picture was of a golden eagle sitting upon a feral cat it had just killed in a ploughed field. It suddenly dawned on me that not only could you fly these creatures, but you also could fly them at prey.

Needless to say, I took both books home and spent the next three days reading them over and over, gleaning every bit of information I possibly could about this wonderful sport and its magnificent birds, including how they were equipped, trained and taught to hunt, and at which quarries they could be flown. One evening, on my father's return from work, I pestered him into taking me into the larger central library in the city. There I was able to find even more books about this fascinating subject, and spent the next few weeks transported to the mountains and Glens of Scotland, or the deserts of Iraq, flying all manner of exotic and exciting birds of prey.

After a month of dedicated reading, I was a self-proclaimed expert, able to quote the various techniques employed by falconers from Russia to Thailand, the bird species they used (both common and Latin names) and the type of quarries hunted. There was no question, I had to get a bird!

I rang up a noted falconer of the time, Philip Glasier, and asked, in what I thought was a very mature way, how an eight-year-old might go about acquiring a peregrine falcon. From what I had read, they appeared to be the most desirable bird to fly. Mr. Glasier is, sadly, no longer with us, but his pointed reply will stay with me forever.

"The chances of a child like you acquiring such a sought-after and prestigious bird are slim to none; you have more chance of riding a unicorn in this year's Derby," he remarked dryly.

When I told my father about the phone call, I was given a "thick-ear," first for bothering such a high-profile gentleman, and second for making an expensive long-distance phone call without permission. Nevertheless, young boys can be particularly determined once they get a bee in their bonnet, and I for one was not about to give up on getting a bird without a fight. I plastered my bedroom walls with posters and pictures cut out of books (sorry to any librarian who is still missing books on falconry) and spent my every waking hour talking, eating and sleeping falconry.

After six long months, my perseverance paid off, and my father, who had been obviously worn down, began making inquiries regarding birds of prey and eventually discovered somebody who bred European kestrels (*Falco tinninculus*). After making a large flight in the garden—which consisted of an eight-foot (2.4-m) by eight-foot (2.4-m) shed adjacent to a chicken-wire area of approximately the same dimensions (a completely unsuitable one in hindsight as you will learn in Chapter 5: Housing Your Raptor)—we set off to collect my very first falconry bird. Thirty years, and many hundreds of birds later, I can still remember coming face to face with my first bird, a kestrel. The defiant eyes, the bloom on feathers, the sharp and menacing-looking beak.

We returned home with Ruby, as we decided to call her, and placed her in the new flight. A couple of days to settle in, one old motorcycle jacket hacked up to make home-made equipment (see Chapter 6: Equipment), and I was ready to "jess" (place leather straps around the bird's legs, which allow the falconer to control the bird) her for the first time. I followed an almost clinical procedure, and in slightly less than an hour she was equipped and unceremoniously placed on my welder's gloved fist.

After sifting through information from many books, the training began in earnest, and within three days she was jumping to my fist (very quick for a kestrel). My dream come true quickly shattered when, for no apparent reason, she started to scream. And scream and scream and scream, even at night! I flipped through book after book and eventually discovered that birds either taken too early from their parents or not reared by their parents (I suspected the latter in Ruby's case) became "imprinted" on their handler (believe that humans are their parents or food providers) and screamed whenever hungry for food. What was I to do? In desperation, I called the well-known falconer I had bothered once before.

"I realise that you have trained many birds of prey and may be able to help me with a problem I am experiencing with my kestrel," I said hesitantly. "She appears to be imprinted and will not stop screaming. What can I do?"

"Ring her bloody neck!" His advice was rather unexpected and obviously never followed.

I think it should be mentioned here that the late Mr. Glasier was of the old school of falconry and firmly believed (quite rightly so) that this is not a sport in which a small child should meddle.

Fortunately, Ruby soon became very tame and began to fly free. A few more weeks and she was very strong on the wing, following me on my bike around a local park each day, coming in to the fist for choice tidbits. After a couple of months, the novelty of flying her to my fist had worn off; I yearned to start hunting with her.

I knew that kestrels tend to hunt smaller mammals like voles and field mice, but I also learned that they sometimes hunt small birds, too, especially those kestrels with young to feed. In vain, I stalked up to feeding groups of sparrows and starlings, throwing Ruby with great encouragement, only to be disappointed time after time. My first official kill in falconry came about six months later, ironically after having completely given up on the thought of hunting with Ruby.

She was as fit as a wild kestrel by then, flying for two or three hours a day. She was so steady and tame that I would just release her for a couple of hours each day to explore the area, ending up at her favourite tree for her daily rations of food. Her trademark hovering was superb; she was able to maintain her position in the air for up to fifteen minutes.

While watching one of her marathon hovers one day, I saw her dive onto a bank and, rather than return to the air moments later, remain on terra firma. Walking over, I noted her furious "mantling" (covering her prey with wings and tail). By "making in" (approaching the bird), I was able to remove a half-eaten frog from her grasp in exchange for food. The first kill! Not a large, memorable one, I'll grant you, but in official terms my bird, bred in captivity and trained by my own fair hand, had made a legitimate kill. I was a falconer (or so I thought at the time!).

Sadly, just over a year later, Ruby did not return from one of her daily sorties and was never seen again. I would like to think that she returned to the wild, found a mate and lived a happy life, but the reality at that time was that there were many young morons with air rifles who shot at anything that stayed still long enough.

My second bird was a sparrow-hawk (*Accipter nisus*), with which I really had my work cut out. This was not the easy imprinted kestrel I had been used to, but a bird that required hard "manning" time (humanisation), "carriage" (training time) and real attention to detail. At first the differences were just too much, and I was convinced that this tiny hawk was untrainable. Three weeks later, I appeared to be no further ahead in my efforts.

So I read a book called *A Hawk for the Bush*, by Jack

Gyr Falcon / *Falco rusticolus.*

Mavrogodato, which still remains in my opinion one of the finest books ever written on the manning and psychology of training a bird of prey. He wrote of "constructive manning," meaning to only handle the bird when it feeds and prolonging the feedings using "tirings" (tougher pieces of food). Using these, what were considered more advanced, methods of training, I was able to eventually fly this bird free and even have a moderate amount of hunting success in the field. Subsequent birds became more and more successful, and by the age of sixteen I had flown around twelve birds and amassed far more experience.

On leaving school, I was faced, like many adolescents, with the prospect of choosing a career, but in what? Many of my friends were going into the local industries of engineering. And like many of the more enigmatic students, my careers' officer bludgeoned my dreams of game-keeping or forestry commission work into reality. I started an engineering apprenticeship the following month.

I look back on this period of my life as my darkest years. I started work at 6:00 a.m. before it got light and returned home at 5:00 p.m. I hated working inside the hot factories, with ultraviolet glows from overhead lights that seemed to suck out my very soul. To add to my misery, I was unable to practise my passion for falconry, mainly a winter sport, for three years. Something had to change.

At this time, I met my future wife, a country girl who rode horses daily and hunted regularly. We soon started to make future plans, all revolving around working in some way in the countryside. In desperation I changed professions and became a travelling salesman, which allowed me more time and, more importantly, daylight to practise my passion.

I then managed to obtain a goshawk and was flying it at weekends (a very unsatisfactory arrangement) with a small amount of success. On one of my weekend forays, I met a breeder of goshawks, peregrines and merlins. He ran his own business and had a wonderful home in the Peak District (a wonderfully scenic part of Derbyshire). Our friendship developed, and I eventually ended up giving up my job and started working for him on a part-time basis, training, caring for and assisting in breeding these birds. From a financial point of view, I was earning a fraction of my original wage, but being out in the country doing what I loved made up for it.

An opportunity then arose to help out at a Scottish Falconry School for a short period, so, going ahead of my wife to establish camp, I packed up a few meagre possessions and headed north of the border. This part-time job turned into a full-time job, and I eventually secured the head falconer position. It was hard, laborious work, often spending upwards of eighteen hours a day with my nose to the grindstone. But I was flying species of birds I had only dreamt about. Plus, I was flying them on land, with much more game than was available back home. I was in my element.

After a couple of seasons, my skills had been honed, my knowledge had increased, but unfortunately my bank balance hadn't. The realities of rearing my first child loomed and I had to find better paying work. One of the country's leading falconry schools was advertising for a head falconer. I applied and was lucky enough to be offered the position. The school's hunting ground was out of this world, the salary was much better and the facility was far superior. It was probably here, more so than anywhere else I had worked, that I was able to fully develop my skills as a professional falconer, honing my techniques to a high standard. At this point I had been working as a professional falconer for five years, earning very little. Now my eyes were fully opened to the success possible for an individual with skill, motivation and a desire to succeed.

I began toying with plans to open a very grand corporate falconry business, whose main objective was to mimic the halcyon days of the "Old Hawking Club." Good food, high-quality sport at venues throughout the country, flying all manner of birds and traditional quarries for very exclusive guests. I was lacking only one key ingredient to make it work … the £500,000 it would take to set up!

At this time, I met a customer who owned a very large business. He had pots of money and was fanatical about field sports of any kind so I showed him my plans. Before I knew it, I was running the falconry business of my dreams. We eventually built up our collection to more than 100 birds, everything from Bonelli's eagles to gyr falcons, which were flown at all manner of quarry. We had our own sporting estate where game was managed to provide superb sport for everything from game hawking to hare hawking. An indication of the estate's quality was my ability, in the first full season, to catch (in fine style) more than 200 pheasants with one falcon!

After four years, the investor's interest drained, and after several arguments, I left. For the first time in my mature life I was unemployed. I decided it was time to start a less ambitious business of my own. After a speculative investment of £2,000 and five years of hard work, my wife and I now manage a falconry business that employs six people, with more than 140 birds in our collection. We now hunt with birds of prey six days per week!

One aspect of my business is to teach falconry to eager beginners. As a professional falconer, I see new people taking up the sport with little or no idea of what they are committing themselves to. More than ever before, I come across birds that are poorly presented, dirty or smashed up as a result of ignorance and a failing in the British legal system to license this sport properly.

Rather than running ineffective one-week courses, each year we accept six clients on a year-long "apprenticeship." (I decided several years ago that it is impossible to learn falconry from a one-week course, indeed it is not even possible to learn it to any standard in a month.) The apprentices come to my facility as often as they can on a weekly basis (usually about two days because of work commitments). During the year, they get to experience what the life of a falconer is like, from breeding to hunting to moulting. By the end of the apprenticeship, they realise the amount of work and dedication it requires to practise the sport well. Many don't even end up getting their own bird, as they realise they cannot do the sport justice.

This book began as a series of course notes to accompany the apprenticeship scheme, but grew and grew until it eventually merited being published in its own right as a beginner's guide to falconry. In writing this book, I wish to share my knowledge and experience in an attempt to assist beginners and their standards of practice through education, hopefully making them strive for greater results.

I have purposely avoided overusing technical falconry words, which I find only serve to confuse the beginner, replacing them with simpler terms. I also based most of the information on training a Harris hawk, a very good choice for a beginner's first bird. Not everything you read in this book will necessarily work for you, of course, but it will give you enough insight to train your first bird to a very high standard, and give you a basis on which to further your skill and knowledge.

— A.J. Hallgarth

PART 1

WELCOME TO FALCONRY

Chapter 1

Objectives of Falconry

Before taking up the sport of falconry, beginners must be clear of their outlying objectives, which will likely include the following:

- I want to hunt wild game with a trained bird of prey.
- I want to mimic my bird's wild counterpart, in appearance and performance.
- I want to practise this sport to the highest possible standard.

Whatever your motivation to start falconry, all would-be falconers should strive to practise falconry to a high standard.

1.1 Plan out your intentions

The first step in practising falconry to a high standard is to plan out your intentions and expectations in light of the realities of falconry.

For instance, realise that falconry is predominantly a winter, daytime sport. Can you spend a minimum of one hour in daylight each day with your bird throughout the winter? Do you have enough space and money to build the minimum standard of accommodation expected? Can you dedicate the next twenty years of your life to this sport? (Your bird could easily live this long.)

If the answer to any of these questions is no, then this sport is not for you. If you are still curious, but don't want the commitment, there are several good falconry schools in the United Kingdom and a few being developed in the United States where you can go to hunt with birds of prey on a daily basis, without the commitment of owning and caring for your own bird.

1.2 Learning by example

If you answered all of the above questions with a resounding yes, what is the best way for you to begin the learning process? The very best way to learn this sport is, in fact, by allying yourself to a practising falconer.

But choosing a falconer is not always easy. Many falconers here in the United Kingdom are unfortunately self-taught and many, I am sad to say, do not practise the sport to a high standard. The sport of falconry almost died out, especially in the West, with the advent of the firearm. With the firearm came a loss of tradition and skill.

In the United Kingdom in particular, we are realising a degeneration of the sport. Once leaders in the field for several hundred years, our standards are now dropping to an all-time low, whilst our American cousins are making great progress with new techniques and psychologies, mainly due to what I consider to be a superior licensing system. Beginners in the United States must apprentice under a falconer for licensure, for example, as falconers did 100 years ago. These falconers served a lengthy and arduous apprenticeship under a more experienced master falconer, who himself underwent similar training in a time when skills were passed from father to son.

Nevertheless, all is not lost here in the United Kingdom; there are still falconers around whom I consider to be among the best in the world, albeit they are in the minority. So, when looking for a mentor, how is a beginner to know a good falconer from a bad one?

I have a few rules that have served me well over the years, proving fairly accurate when assessing the ability of so-called "experts." They are as follows:

- What condition is their bird in? Are its feathers perfect at the end of the hunting season or smashed up?
- What condition is their "mews" (the name for the building in which a falcon or hawk is housed) in? Is it clean enough to eat your dinner from or is it and their equipment dirty and unhygienic?
- Are they analytical? Are they able to break down particular bird behaviour into segments or are they complacent?
- Does their bird perform to expectation? Or is there a reason why it hasn't performed yet again?
- Do they catch much of the quarry they set out to hunt?

If you meet a falconer who can fulfil all of these requirements, then beg, plead, pay him or her to train you.

1.3 Other ways to learn

There are many commercial falconry centres that offer residential courses as well. Some courses advertised can be as short as a week. Unfortunately, you cannot learn such a complex and involved sport as this in one week; you would, in fact, struggle to learn enough in one month. Most enterprises of this type make a living from performing demonstrations to their public visitors. Courses, as an afterthought, are a way for falconry centres to make extra money at times of the year when business is not as good.

So what are your alternatives? Some people may say "join a club" and visit a field meet. I would agree wholeheartedly that joining a club is beneficial (see Contacts of Interest). These organisations will represent you from a political standpoint, but need your subscriptions to do so. The other benefits of joining a club may be many and varied, such as:

- Insurance (a must in this day and age in the United Kingdom).
- Subsidised registration of birds (in the United Kingdom).
- Club breeding programmes.
- Newsletters and information.
- Governmental representation of our sport.

But be warned: membership in a club here in the United Kingdom doesn't automatically make that person an expert.

A final alternative is to read and absorb a very good book. Many beginners, however, read several books at the same time, each one contradicting the other in some small way, leaving the reader confused. It's best to stick to one good author and, since you are already reading this book, it might as well be this one. All the information you will require to house, equip, train, care for and manage your first bird (I suggest a Harris hawk or perhaps a red-tail for beginners) is contained in these pages. Read this book from cover to cover, absorb it, then read it again before you even think of getting a bird. As my grandfather used to say, "The only thing you'll get by rushing is a baby!"

Chapter 2

Legalities of the Sport

Now that you've decided you want to take up falconry, you should be aware of the legalities of the sport. The law in the United Kingdom is fickle when it comes to falconry. U.K. laws regarding falconry change on an almost daily basis. Because of the frequent changes to these laws, you should check with your local Department for Environment, Food and Rural Affairs (DEFRA) offices, at the time you take up the sport. In the meantime, there are some current laws that are worth discussing.

2.1 U.K. laws

At the time of writing, U.K. laws require that most birds used for falconry must be bred in captivity; using wild birds for this sport is not permitted, unless they fall into one of two categories: birds taken under licence before 1986, or birds intended and held under special licence for rehabilitation.

The rarer or more sensitive species are identified by a numbered ring on their leg (either from DEFRA or the breeder). These birds fall into a category called "Schedule 4." All Schedule 4 birds are legally required to be registered with DEFRA in the United Kingdom. There is a registration fee, and re-registration occurs every three years.

In addition to registration, owners must also carry a European Union (EU) document called an "Article 10." This document is issued to the breeder at the time the bird is bred and should remain with the bird throughout its life. The Article 10 document lists the purposes for which the bird may be used.

If you keep Schedule 4 birds, you may be inspected from time to time by a DEFRA representative (or Scottish Executive in Scotland) to ensure the bird in your care is registered correctly.

Certain sensitive species (Schedule 4) birds may originate from the wild through injury or accident, but, again, these birds will have been issued with some form of identification, either a cable tie ring or a Swiss ring, and will also be required to carry a microchip if they are part of a breeding project.

Non-sensitive species do not require registration or Article 10 documents if they are not being used for any commercial purpose. Still, you should be able to prove, if questioned, where they came from. For most non-Schedule 4 birds, this takes the form of a *Declaration of Captive Breeding*, which is your proof that the bird in your possession did not come from the wild.

This declaration is given by the breeder of the bird and should state the bird's means of identification, its parents' means of identification and the date it hatched. Most importantly, it must contain the sentence: "And was bred by me, from parent birds legally held in my possession at that time." The breeder should then sign the declaration with his or her full name, address and date.

The birds of this category do not legally require a numbered ring, but it is advantageous for them to either carry a ring or be microchipped by your veterinarian as a means of identification.

So, if you intend to obtain a bird in the United Kingdom, you are looking for one bred in captivity from a reputable breeder who is willing to issue you a *Declaration of Captive Breeding*. As long as you can meet these criteria, all you need is enough money to buy the bird! I hope it's only those serious about the sport who do so.

2.2 U.S. laws and permits

In the United States, the legalities of the sport change from state to state, but in general the laws relating to bird of prey ownership and welfare are fortunately much stricter than in the United Kingdom. For example, some states require that you build your accommodation to their minimum specifications and will even inspect said accommodation to see that it reaches their minimum standards before a permit is issued.

In some states, it is necessary to take a written basic knowledge test to show that you are competent in and aware of what you are getting into. U.S. federal laws prohibit you from flying some of the more difficult species until your skill level matches their more demanding requirements. You should contact your local wildlife agency to learn about the falconry laws specific to your state.

There are three main falconry permits available in the United States—the apprentice, general falconer and master falconer permits.

As a U.S. apprentice, you can trap a "passage" (a bird taken from the wild in juvenile plumage) red-tailed hawk, which is a great beginner's bird due to its robust size and nature.

Once a general permit is obtained, certain states allow the use of Harris hawks, which have, in my opinion, greater longevity as a useful falconer's bird.

Eventually, once a master's permit is obtained, the broader spectrum of falconry birds will open up to you, giving you the opportunity to fly some of the most prized and specialised birds such as the gyr falcon and peregrine falcon.

Chapter 3

Time and Place to Train

If you decide to join the sport of falconry, first ensure that you consider the logistics involved, including the time of year appropriate to train your bird.

Look to nature to tell you what time of year to start training your bird. In particular, looking at the way birds of prey time the hatching and developing of their young is a good indicator of when to train your bird.

Take the example of the smaller bird-eating hawks, like the sparrow-hawks or the Cooper's hawks, who nest very late in the year and time the hatch of their eggs with the "fledging" (leaving the nest) of the prey species. By doing so, they can hunt all of these young, inexperienced bird species to feed their ever-hungry brood of young. The sparrow-hawk's growth rate is rapid, reaching mature body size at around six to seven weeks.

Young hawks also spend the next few weeks developing their predatory skills on relatively easy, inexperienced prey. They then develop their predatory skills at a rate to match their prey's defences. For these kind of natural reasons, it is important to start training your young falconry bird at the right time of year.

The exercise is simple: try to mimic the wild birds of prey with timings and development. You'll find that August is a good month to start training a Harris hawk or red-tail, which I've already recommended as good species for beginners to start with.

3.1 Game seasons

Although many people may not realise it, humans have managed game and wildlife for many hundreds, if not thousands, of years. Our ancestors realised that killing birds and animals at times of breeding or rearing young would mean a reduced number of these creatures, and therefore less to hunt or harvest.

It's also important that we do not hunt certain game species at a time when they are reproducing and rearing young for moral reasons. It may be exciting to kill a pheasant for the first time with your bird, but this is no real achievement if it is still a poult and hardly able to fly.

For these reasons, it is important for falconers to conform to the same game seasons as the other members of the hunting fraternity.

It is important for falconers to conform to the same game seasons as the other members of the hunting fraternity.

The game seasons in the United Kingdom are as follows:

- Ptarmigan—August 12 to December 10.
- Red grouse—August 12 to December 10.
- Black grouse—August 20 to December 10.
- Capercaillie—October 1 to January 31.
- Pheasant—October 1 to January 31.
- Partridge—September 1 to February 1.
- Woodcock—September 1 (Scotland) to January 31.
- Snipe—August 12 to January 31.
- Moorhen—September 1 to January 31.
- Coot—September 1 to January 31.
- Hares—no closed season, but they may not be killed on Sundays or Christmas Day.
- Rabbit—no closed season.
- Goose and duck—September 1 to January 31 (extended to February 21 in any area above high-water mark).

Please remember that if you intend to hunt game, it is still a legal requirement here in the United Kingdom to have a game licence purchased for around £12 from any large post office.

Game seasons and bag limits in North America are set by each state or province independently, based on local game populations. Many states have extended falconry seasons (beyond the gun seasons) to reflect the relatively fewer numbers of game taken and to encourage falconers to fly their birds. For example, upland game bird seasons for falconry generally run from September 1 to March 31, with a daily limit of only one or two birds per day. Similar seasons exist for jackrabbits (hares) and cottontail rabbits, but with a more liberal bag limit. Waterfowl and other migratory bird seasons are more restricted due to international treaties with Mexico and Canada, limiting the number of days available for hunting.

3.2 Land on which to fly

Considering the timing for training is clearly important, but so is finding a place to train your birds. Traditionally, falconers in the United Kingdom have sought permission to fly their birds on estate

PART 2

GETTING PREPARED

Chapter 4

Selection of Species

Choosing what type of bird you want to acquire is, without a doubt, the most important decision you, as a beginner, will have to make. In North America, as mentioned, this choice may be made for you. In the United Kingdom, there is more freedom of choice, so beginners must be especially careful to choose prudently. There are many species of birds of prey that can be trained for this sport, but few are actually suitable to the beginner.

Here is a description of the various families of birds. By developing a greater understanding of their evolution in the wild, you can apply that knowledge to assess their suitability to the sport of falconry. However, keep in mind that selection of a species is just the first step in getting prepared to acquire a bird, so don't run out and get a bird just yet.

4.1 The falcons (*Falco*)

These birds are known as the "long-wings," a name they have received because of their long, pointed, blade-like wings. Types of falcons include peregrines and kestrels. Other common characteristics include:

- Long paented wings.
- Toothed or notched beak.
- Dark eyes (appear to be black from a distance).
- Pronounced orbital ridge.
- Malar stripe (the dark stripe under their eyes).

Evolution of Male Versus Female Hawks

The male bird of prey of most species is usually up to one third smaller than the female. This characteristic is known as "sexual dimorphism," and like most things in nature, is not an accident.

When birds of prey nest, it is the female that takes on the more arduous role of incubation of eggs; the male is responsible for the collection of food. He returns to the nest area, offers the female food and then takes over a short role of incubation whilst she feeds.

Because incubation can take anywhere from twenty-eight to forty-eight days, the male will need to hunt in close proximity of the nest site. This puts the available prey species in that area in an unbelievable amount of pressure and could result in the total extermination of certain prey species. So, nature in her wisdom provides sexual dimorphism as the answer. The smaller male is slightly faster and more manoeuvrable, making certain prey species available to the male bird of prey only. When the eggs hatch and a greater amount of food is required at the nest, the female hunts the larger prey species still available in the area. The combined result is that there are always available prey for either sex.

So, considering the sex of certain species of birds can be quite important in your selection process. If, for example, you wish to hunt male pheasant with a tiercel or male peregrine, you are going to have your work cut out for you; the female is far better suited to this stronger quarry.

Likewise, when selecting the sex of a Harris hawk, you'll find males need to be dropped much lower in weight when initially entering on rabbit. Would you take on something larger than yourself?

This is not the case with the red-tail, where both sexes are of sufficient size to take rabbit with ease. But female red-tails are more powerful, so a male is a better choice for a beginner, who may be overawed by the female's prowess.

Note the size difference between a juvenile male and a mature, female Harris hawk.

A peregrine falcon.

- Long, spindly toes.
- Medium to short tail length.

Their eye colour, orbital ridge and malar stripe are all adaptations in nature that are specific to their vision. Having a large eye is a distinct advantage when hunting in bright light, especially when backed up with a pronounced orbital ridge, which allows the eye to be shaded further from bright light. The malar stripe is also a very clever adaptation, reflecting or deflecting bright light away from the eye. Some American football players use black wax under their eyes in a similar way to avoid the dazzle of the stadium lights!

The falcon's toothed beak allows them to break the necks of small prey very efficiently.

In aviation, any object, which sticks out from the fuselage, creates drag. In this way falcons, similarly to fighter aircraft, can swing their wings closer to their bodies, reducing drag and increasing air-

wood. Although easy to work with, it has a limited life expectancy, needs regular maintenance and is very hard to keep sanitary.

In this day and age, with timber being the price it is, it's nearly as cheap to build in concrete block, which requires no maintenance, can be kept hygienic, and is cool in the summer and warmer in the winter. (It also safeguards the trees in the habitat of many rainforest birds and animals!)

A concrete mews can be painted or tiled, and the outside, with a little gardening skill, can be blended very well into its environment.

The internal surface areas of your free-loft area will, no matter how carefully you position your perches, get mutes on them, which are very hard to clean off. If money were no object, you could line the walls with Perspex or perhaps tile. A cheaper alternative is to line them with polythene sheets, which are easy to clean and can be replaced very inexpensively from time to time.

5.4 Roof

With solid walls, you will need as much natural light as possible. I actually prefer to leave my roofs half-meshed (the bird can't fly into the mesh on the roof easily), allowing the bird some access to the weather. You'll be amazed at the conditions in which your bird will sit out braving the elements.

Some people like to use modern roof materials like Onduline, but in my opinion it does not age well and tends to sag or even puncture. I like to use plywood covered with the old reliable roof felt. If money were of no object, I would choose plastic-coated, aluminium profile sheets.

Remember also to allow for snow loading on the roof and build a sufficient pitch or angle to allow water to run off.

5.5 Perches

Birds made to sit on the same perch day in and day out are a little like invalids who are bedridden—they get sores. For a person, regular turning and repositioning can treat these sores, but this is not possible for a bird.

Falcon perched on Astroturf-topped block.

The sores on a bird's feet can become infected, quickly turning into bumblefoot or pododermatitis (see Chapter 19: Health and First Aid). A modern way to help prevent such ailments is the use of materials like rubber or Astroturf.

Rubber, such as sections of knobbly bike tire, can be fastened to a perch so that every time the bird moves its feet, the pressure points are changed, avoiding any chance of foot inflammation. Astroturf is also excellent for this, although it is harder to clean, especially if pieces of food jam into its fibres.

The more perches you place in your loose loft, the more areas of potential mutes you will have to clean. I like to position my perches at different heights, starting with the lowest at the food station and the highest at the window. This will encourage your bird to work a little harder when flying up from the food station to the window. This makes the bird exercise more at times like the moult when there is a remote danger of building higher cholesterol. In addition, position some of the perches in an area of the chamber that will allow them to sunbathe, but equally in warmer climates, make sure they also have shade.

Sometimes young birds or breeding birds like to lie down (very unusual in older birds), so it does not hurt to provide an area for this purpose. A flat ledge covered with gravel is suitable for this purpose.

5.6 Food station

When a bird is moulting (see Chapter 20: The Moult), there should be a minimum of disturbance in the free-lofting area. For this reason, a food chute can be positioned in the wall, allowing you to feed the bird without going in.

The food lands on a platform from which the bird can collect it. Because this platform is an obvious point of disease or potential infection, it is necessary to keep it especially clean.

I have designed my own platforms that are basically timber-framed wire trays. Because the surface area in which the foot comes into contact with the wire is lowered, so is the chance of disease. The

Food chute. (Note wire collection tray edged with Astroturf, on which the bird stands to reach the food.)

platforms can also be sprayed daily with Virkon (see Chapter 19: Health and First Aid), which keeps them sanitary without pollution.

5.7 Windows

Some people like to look at their birds regularly when free lofted. I would imagine that the birds themselves would like a view of some sort when in the chamber. The site and position of a window in the chamber is actually very important.

A conventional glass window cannot be used as your bird is likely to fly into the glass; a vertically barred window is preferable (your bird would try to sit on horizontal bars, causing great feather damage). For the bars, I use plastic, half-inch (1.3-cm) overflow pipe,

A vertical-barred chamber window.

which I position approximately two inches (5 cm) apart. If a bird does fly into these, they have a small degree of flex that acts like a sponge absorbing some of the shock. Chamber bars made of soft PVC hollow pipe allow for some degree of flex.

A note of caution: a friend of mine used an old glass window in his new mews, and placed electrical tape in vertical strips down the glass to make what appeared to be a barrier to his bird. On the second day that his bird was free lofted, it flew into and broke the glass, breaking its neck!

Birds like elevation and feel much more secure when they are at the highest point. Therefore, the window needs to be fairly high up on the wall, rather than at eye level as humans prefer.

5.8 Weathering yard

A weathering area is basically an area in which a bird can be tethered to its perch to partake of the weather and is protected from predators.

It will become apparent, when reading the training sections of this book, that you will need to tether your bird at various stages of its life. Some people try to use their free-lofting chamber for this purpose, but this does have downsides. If a bird is tethered in such a position and can see higher perches above, it will "bate" (i.e., jump off the perch) repeatedly to reach them (often resulting in feather damage).

Equally, if you have just removed your bird from moulting and are tethering it to retrain, it will have favourite perches and the same problems arise. It can sometimes be handy to have somewhere to tie your bird whilst you clean out its free-lofting chamber. And if a fellow falconer spends some time at your place with his or her bird, this extra space can be very handy.

The ideal weathering area should have several key components:

- A soft floor surface that is not only sanitary and easy to clean, but also kind to feathers if the tethered bird should bate; pea-gravel is ideal.
- Enough space to allow the bird to bate without contacting any part with wings or tail feathers.
- Shade from sun, or protection from rain and snow.

opening just as human heads and mouths do. So when ordering your hood, if you ask nicely, the manufacturer may send you three hoods, one slightly larger, the other smaller. Try on all three and send back the ones that don't fit. Note that if you bite the hood braces at this stage, you will mark them and probably be asked to pay for them.

If for some reason you are unhappy with them all, please don't force your bird to wear a hood that may be too tight or touches its eyes. You'll only make it hood shy, refusing to accept it in future.

If a hood appears to fit well at first, keep it on for a couple of minutes, then look at the area around the eyes for signs of moisture, a sure sign that the hood is touching the eyes. If there is moisture, the hood does not fit properly.

If you do not have a suitable hood for your new bird, loose-loft your bird in its mews, put your training programme on hold and wait for the arrival of replacements.

With all this said, you're probably wondering how you actually go about hooding the bird for the first time. Hooding is probably one of the most difficult skills that a beginner has to learn; much like riding a bike, it requires practice—the more you do it, the better you get. It's easy for the beginner to give up on hooding, so please persevere. The benefits far outweigh the disadvantages for both you and bird. If you start early enough or can practise on a bird already well made to the hood, then you will have a running start.

Unfortunately, this practice has to be carried out on a young bird who, if badly hooded will become hood shy and very difficult to hood in the future. It has to be said that a bird that has never been hooded is far easier to hood than a bird that has had several aborted attempts made.

The act of getting your hood on the bird's head, if done correctly, is the easy part. Hold your hood between finger and thumb by its plume, with the opening of the hood upwards.

Stroke the breast of your bird slowly with the neck strap of the hood.

The next stage is where a lot of people go wrong. Up to this point, you have been moving slowly and deliberately

Stroking your bird with the neck strap of the hood.

Moving the hood slowly up the breast, with an aim to axis under the chin.

The hood seating is put into place on the head.

whilst dealing with your bird. It is important that you do the same when putting the hood on your bird's head. Many people try to rush at this stage. Imagine that the centre of the hood's chinstrap is a hinge, which when in contact with the underside of the beak allows the hood to rotate onto your bird's head.

As soon as the hood is on the head, let go! Don't try to hold on. If the hood isn't on all the way, gently push against the plume with the tips of your fingers. Now you've achieved the easy part. It's now time to fasten the hood. Place the nearest, longest hood brace loosely into your mouth (do not allow the bird to feel the pressure in any way).

The next step has to happen literally all at once. Take the opposite hood brace in your hand and draw it tight against the other, whilst pushing your fist and bird up and forwards.

This action pulls the hood onto the head whilst it is fastened. If you keep the fist still at this stage, the bird will just lean backwards leaving you with a closed hood between your teeth and fingers, and an unhooded bird! This is a difficult operation and requires practice.

If possible, try to practise on someone else's bird that is already well made to its hood, even if it requires paying a commer-

The braces are drawn between teeth and hand.

A happy hooded Harris hawk on a perch.

cial falconry centre or school. The instruction you will receive on the school's birds will prevent you from making a mess of your own. It will be money well spent! At the very least, ask a friend to provide a bent finger, onto which you must fasten a hood. Ask them to make it a little difficult by moving or trying to pull it back out of the hood at crucial moments. It may sound strange, but this will really help your technique.

6.2 Perches

Certain species of birds have evolved to sit on certain types of perches. Hawks living in woodland have a foot that is designed to wrap around a tree branch. Falcons, on the other hand, spend most of their lives in open country on cliff and rock and have a larger,

The bow perch.

flatter foot better suited to a flat surface. For these reasons, a variety of perches have evolved in falconry. Below are discussions of two of the many perches commonly used by falconers: the bow perch and the block.

6.2.1 The bow perch

In medieval times, man hunted with both archery bow and hawk, often both at the same time. When perching, all birds of prey like to sit at the highest point. With this knowledge, ancient falconers discovered that the bow shape, pressed firmly into the ground, allowed their birds both wing and tail clearance, as well as comfort.

Before the initial purchase of a bow perch, you need to decide whether you intend to use it in inside or out. There are two basic designs available, either a spiked bow or a weighted foot bow. (There are even designs that allow you both options interchangeably.)

I find a well-made stainless weighted bow fills all of my requirements as it can be used on any surface and remains portable. Mild steel is strong but does not weather. It can be anodised or galvanised but with bangs and hard wear, the protective coating will chip off, allowing it to rust. Stainless steel is much better and will last a lifetime, but it is obviously more expensive.

Note that if you choose a weighted foot perch, a smooth foot will allow the perch to be dragged more easily than one that has rubber feet. If your bird is to be tethered in close proximity of others, your bird may be able drag its bow perch to reach another bird, resulting in disaster. (See Chapter 5: Housing Your Raptor for more information on choosing a surface on which to place your perch.)

The tethering ring on your bow should be of a strong but light material. It should also be large enough to slip easily over the diameter of the bow without snagging.

6.2.2 The block perch

Birds with a flat foot prefer to sit on blocks. As Harris hawks and red-tails have feet designed to cling around branches, they are more comfortable on bow perches, but some people like to use blocks.

When choosing the size of block, consider the size of the bird. Many people think that providing the largest block size available is kinder to their bird. Wrong! Your block should be sufficiently large that your bird can sit with both feet on top and still have tail overhanging the side. Larger blocks encourage your bird to sit more centrally, resulting in their mute covering its surface.

A block with straight sides allows the bird to smear mute all over it. So choose a block type that gradually decreases in diameter from its top. Note also that the more elaborate the grooves and steel work, the harder they are to clean. Plain and simple is best.

Wooden blocks require regular maintenance and may split in cold weather. There are, however, composite plastic and fibreglass options now available that are more durable and offer greater longevity.

Your jess length is also very important when using a block. If your jess is longer than the diameter of your block, they will eventually slip over, or "straddle," the block, and your bird may get tangled, upset and possibly even break feathers.

The tethering position is also an important consideration when choosing a style of block. I really dislike using the Arab-style blocks, which, although beautiful, tend to have very small tethering rings at the base, which will repeatedly

A hooded "hybrid" falcon on a block perch.

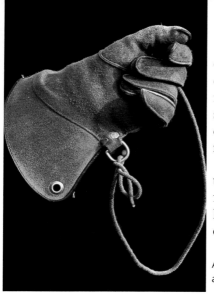

clog up the leash (resulting in feather damage). The Arab system of tethering is different to that which I subscribe, so these blocks aren't really designed for use with Western equipment.

Based on my experience, I prefer the traditional block, which if manufactured correctly allows freedom of leash and equipment, practicality of cleaning and aesthetic good looks.

An ideal gauntlet for a male red-tail or a Harris hawk.

6.3 Glove or gauntlet

There are many qualities of glove, or gauntlet, available. They differ in style from manufacturer to manufacturer, but as a rule I always tend to go for quite a high-cuff length glove, preferably double-thickness and made of buckskin. If you are considering the training of large female red-tail, then I strongly suggest a double- or even triple-thickness buckskin glove.

I especially prefer a glove that has hand-stitched fingers. When sewing machines stitch leather, they make neat stitching, but they tend to group these stitches very close together. This makes the leather closely perforated, much like the tear in toilet paper. Because the fingers bend and wear quicker than the rest, this increases the chances of the glove splitting around the fingers. This is less likely to happen with a hand-stitched glove, which do, however, tend to be a little more expensive.

Obviously if you fly merlins or sparrow hawks, a larger glove would be an overkill, but as I recommend you consider training a Harris hawk or red-tail, then you may need a glove that can withstand a more powerful grip.

Also, the glove should be fitted with a strong metal tethering "D" ring, which is well stitched or riveted to the glove. Your glove when the bird is in the mews and tethered, but when free flown, this mews jess can be removed and replaced with a flying jess, basically an identical jess but without the slit for the swivel.

The benefits of this system of jess are obvious, preventing your bird from becoming entangled in trees when flown. The only bad point to "Aylmeri" jesses are the bracelets.

If you are flying a bird that has a tendency to bate, or jump around a lot, when tethered (especially common in short-wings), the brass eyelets can inflame the back of the ankles, eventually resulting in damage and infection. This does not happen with the traditional jess, as there is no item that is made from metal involved in its construction.

The final type of jess you could use is the "false Aylmeri." This system employs the best parts of both jess types; the bracelets are bound onto the bird's legs using the same method as the traditional jess, but they do employ a brass eyelet that is positioned further away from the bird's legs (avoiding inflammation). Because it has an eyelet, this then allows you to utilise and change both mews and flying jesses.

The only fault I have found with the false Aylmeri is that if they are badly manufactured, they leave the eyelet very close to the bird's rear talon and toe. If the talon slips into the eyelet and the bird bates, it can result in a broken toe.

Although the Aylmeri bracelet system allows you to interchange jess, from mews to flying, I personally have experienced many problems in the hunting field when birds playing with their flying jess are able to remove and lose them.

I now use a permanent system of flying jess in the form of a small slip of leather fastened around the bracelet that is virtually impossible for the bird to remove in the flying field.

Other equipment you need to manufacture jesses include:
- good-quality hide, preferably Kangaroo skin.
- scissors.
- metal rule.
- scalpel.
- eyelet tool with eyelets.
- artery clamp or pliers.
- leather dressing/jess grease.
- leather hole punch.

Equipment needed for manufacturing jesses.

So let us look at how to manufacture some Aylmeri jesses.

Cut two strips of leather, stretching the hide first and cutting in the direction of the least stretch. They should be about 2 mm (.08 in) wider than the brass eyelets and at least 30-cm (1-ft) long.

Rub leather dressing/jess grease liberally into the leather, ensuring that it is well worked in. Wipe off any excess.

Cut a point on one end of each strip of leather, squaring the opposite end off.

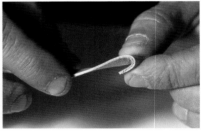

Start to fold the square end of the leather approximately the same width as the brass eyelet (not smaller).

Fold the leather three times to form the button.

Using your leather punch, punch a hole through the centre of the button.

Pinch the pointed end of the strap together (suede side inwards); a push point through punched hole in button.

Draw the strap through the hole either by hand or with the use of artery forceps/pliers until the button is tight.

To prepare the Aylmeri bracelets, cut two strips of leather about 2 mm (.08 in) wider than the brass eyelets you will use, grease as before and place the eyelet centrally at one end (allowing for all-around overlap). Make an impression and then punch out this hole using your leather punch. Test eyelet for size and trim around it with scissors, allowing a 1 mm (.04 in) overhang.

Begin to cut a fringe by making small parallel insertions in the size of the bracelet for about 3 cm (1.2 in). (These may be finished once you size the bird's leg and are ready to fit the bracelets). To prepare permanent flying straps/jess, cut two strips of leather about 30-cm (1-ft) long and 4-mm (.16-in) wide. Cut a sharp point on one end and grease, punching a small hole in the other end.

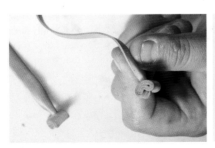

The finished button(s). / Decide how long your jess needs to be (e.g., no longer in length than the diameter of a block perch or no longer than 15 cm (.5 ft) for a Harris hawk.) Cut a fresh point at the desired length, and then punch a small hole at the top and the bottom of the 3-cm (1.2-in) slit that will accommodate the swivel.

6.6 Swivel

The swivel is connected to the jess and allows the jess to be utilised without tangling. There are various types of swivels, made from various metals. I would recommend the use of a stainless-steel swivel.

The benefit of the flat-top type swivel will become apparent with use; when you fasten your jess onto your swivel, you will find that ordinary swivels allow your jess to slip down, eventually jamming the swivel's action and allowing your bird to tangle up (which may result in feather damage).

Some falconers prefer to pass one jess onto one side, and the other on the opposite side, but I personally prefer to pass them both over the same side, as this helps to keep them together and stops them from slipping down.

There are some equipment manufacturers, who have incorporated a rubber system into their swivels, supposedly eleviating the shock when a bird bates. I favour anything that gives my bird greater comfort, but am unwilling to trust this new device until the strength of rubber can be proven over a prolonged period of time.

The swivel is fitted by placing both pointed ends of the mews jess together and passing them through the larger end of the swivel.

Over the smaller end, bring both sides back up to the bar, finally pulling slightly to seat them onto the top bar of the swivel.

6.7 Leash

Traditionally, leashes were manufactured from leather, but because of its poor reliability in all weathers, I do not trust leather leashes.

In this day and age, human-made materials like braided nylon are incredibly durable and strong, offering the perfect alternative to leather. In these materials your choice is extensive: flat-braided nylon, cotton-coated braided nylon or polypropylene.

I do not like flat leashes, as I find them almost impossible to undo if wet and totally impossible when frozen in winter. Likewise, I do not particularly like polypropylene as it is slippery and awkward to tie. I prefer cotton-coated braided nylon, which is very easy to handle, hard-wearing, and once a leash is made, it should last you a lifetime. See the photos below to learn how to manufacture a leash.

Cut a suitable length of leash material (approximately 80 cm (2.6 ft)) and place one end against your thumb, and start to coil around your thumb.

Start to coil back on itself for four turns. Slide your thumb out and feed the opposite end of the leash down through the centre of the coils. Pull the full leash length through the coils until it forms a knot. Finish the knot end by cutting excess material and melting onto knot with a naked flame. Melt the opposite end to stop it from fraying.

There are now elasticised or Bungee leashes on the market. The idea behind these is that they take the trauma out of a bird's bate, reducing stress to legs. Great idea, but unfortunately for every forward motion there is a backward one, and on the backward bounce, the bird tends to dig its tail into the ground, breaking feathers!

A kinder alternative is to always ensure that you tie your bird as short as possible (without it constantly pulling on its legs). This results in your bird achieving less speed in the bate, therefore being pulled up with less stress.

Once you have made your leash, it is an ideal opportunity to practise tying your falconer's knot, a knot that can be tied or untied using only one hand (you'll have a bird on the other). See photos below to see how to tie a falconer's knot.

Holding the leash's-button in your gloved hand, as though it were your bird; pass the leash end through the tethering ring on your glove.

Place your hand through the loop, take the furthest leash in your first two fingers, leaving your thumb outside.

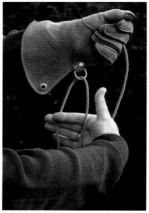

Reach forwards with your thumb and lift the furthest leash, bringing it back against your fingers to form a loop.

Bring the leash in your fingers from behind and over the top of the knot.

Push the leash in your fingers, down through the loop created by your thumb. Drawing your thumb out, pull it up to make a tight loop.

Finally, tuck what remains of your leash back through the loop. This gives you added safety: if the bird plays with the leash, it will only tighten it, rather than undo it. To untie, simply pull the loose end out of the loop and pull!

6.8 Bells

A bell is an audible location device, which has become far less important with the advent of telemetry, but still allows you to locate your bird at close range. When purchasing a bell, you are looking to fulfil three criteria, as follow:

- Tone (can you hear it over a distance?).
- Weight (is it light enough for your bird?).
- Longevity (will it last a whole season?).

The first criteria should be met by all falconry bells. As for the second, manufacturers are starting to produce some very heavy bells, which although hard wearing and long-lasting (over several seasons), they do weigh your bird down slightly. As to the size of a bell, use your common sense; smaller is better provided you can hear them.

As a bell ages, the dropper (piece of metal inside) starts to wear its way through the bell. This changes the tone, and the dropper will eventually break its way out. For this reason I prefer to use an Indian or "Lahore" bell, which has changed very little in design or manufacture for several hundred years. They offer good tone, are reasonably priced and will normally last you a full season.

Bells may be mounted on the leg or tail, but which is preferable? I prefer to use both, placing one bell on a "bewitt" (a piece of leather on the leg) and another on the tail, which also gives me a point to secure the telemetry. The benefit of a leg bell comes into its own when a bird is physically footing or killing its prey; at this time the legs are moving rapidly and can be heard from quite a distance. There are, however, many occasions when a bird is killing in long grass or cover; at this time the leg bell is muffled, and the clearer position of the bell on the tail becomes advantageous.

To make a bewitt, see the following photos.

Cut a strip of leather approximately 3-mm (.12-in) wide by 15-cm (.5-ft) long. Cut a point on both ends and grease. Using your hole punch, punch a small hole in the middle or so of the strap. Insert an end of the strap in the bar of the bell and feed bell to position in the centre.

Place one of the pointed ends of your strap through the hole in the centre and pull through, attaching the strap to the bell.

Finally punch another small hole in the strap approximately 1 cm (.4 in) away from the bell position. This is as far as you can go until it is time to fit it.

The mountain deflects the signal depriving the receiver.

Any obstacles in the area act to deflect this signal, sometimes bouncing at severe angles.

Although a telemetry manufacturer might advertise that its particular transmitter has a thirty-mile (48-km) range, this range will only be within line of sight. Any mountains or buildings might defer this signal in certain circumstances to less than a quarter of a mile.

When using telemetry, try to always use new or relatively new batteries. Practise a lot with your new system. A good way to practise is to get a family member or friend to position your transmitter somewhere a couple of miles away. It's then your job to go and find it. I start off with my receiver gain turned up fully. I then imagine that I am standing at the centre of a clock face. I turn my receiver aerial through the twelve hours of the clock (360 degrees).

Narrow down the strongest signal, into a quarter of the clock face (for example, between twelve and three o'clock) and then turn down the gain until your signal has almost gone. Do not touch or turn up your gain after this.

You are now looking at a certain direction somewhere in a ninety-degree arc, hopefully less. I can tell by the setting of the gain on my receiver approximately how far away my transmitter is.

Head off (either by car or on foot) in the approximate direction of the signal. I would normally go about a quarter of a mile. Stop and repeat the clock face process again. If your signal has got stronger without turning up your gain, then you are obviously going in the right direction. If the signal is coming from the way you have just come, then you have obviously gone too far. Keep repeating this process, gradually turning your gain down, as you get closer. You will eventually get to the point where you have a very strong signal with your gain turned right down. As you walk with your receiver, you will physically see the signal suddenly drop, until you turn 180 degrees and it returns. You are now within a few feet of your transmitter!

Some systems allow you to turn the yaggi aerial part of your receiver off and just use the receiver box on its own—when within three to four feet (.9–1.2 m)—others have fancy attenuators that basically do the same thing. Either way, criss-cross the ground at this stage looking for the strongest signal. Most systems when operated properly will guide you to your transmitter even in the dark! Practise and you will be ready in case you really do need it.

6.11 Scales

When purchasing scales to weigh your bird, you have two main options: balance or digital. I do not like digital scales for the following reasons:

- They are manufactured specifically to weigh inanimate objects. Also, the way in which they are designed to record weight makes any modification to the original design ineffective (e.g., the fitting of a perch).
- They are often light or top heavy, which makes them unstable.
- They will often reset (tare) in the initial stages of a bird stepping on.

I have tried dozens of sets of digital scales from different manufacturers, but as yet have found none that are accurate enough for the purposes of falconry. A scale that is only one quarter of an ounce out could result in the death of a smaller species of hawk.

Balance scales can be heavy, old-fashioned, expensive, but they are a very simple mechanism, which allows very little to go wrong.

A young, hooded Harris hawk on the scales.

You can choose to weigh in ounces or grammes, both of which are accurate if used properly. If you want ultra-sensitive scales, you might like to try the Ohaus dial-a-gram scales, which are accurate to a fraction of a gramme.

You may want to convert your own scale, as many old candy-shop type scales can be purchased from second-hand bric-a-brac shops.

6.12 Weighing charts

The importance of weighing and monitoring your bird's weight during training and flying will become apparent throughout the remainder of this book. As well as columns to record actual weight, your chart will also need columns to record time of weighing, food intake, food type, temperature on the day, weather condition (is your bird heavy because it is wet?) and finally your personal remarks so that you can record performance and look back upon it in future months.

Bird's Name: *Baldrick*				Species: ♂ *Harris Hawk*		Ring Number: *1234W*
Date	Weight	Time	Intake	Foodtype/type	Temp.	Remarks
23/4	1lb. 9¼ oz.	10 am	3 oz.	rabbit	7°	Flew ok, caught 1 rabbit.
24/4	1lb. 9 oz.	12 noon	3 oz.	chick	6°	Not flown.
25/4	1lb. 9 oz.	12 noon	3 oz.	chick	6°	Little slow to respond.
26/4	1lb. 9 oz.	11 am	1 oz.	chick	6°	Very slow to fist, need to drop.
27/4	1lb. 8½ oz.	1 pm	2 oz.	chick	7°	Bit better, still a little lazy.
28/4	1lb. 8¼ oz.	12 noon	3 oz.	chick	7°	Great! 1 pheasant, flew very well.
20/4	1lb. 8¼ oz.	1 pm	3 oz.	pheasant	6°	Very, very good.

A sample weight chart and graph.

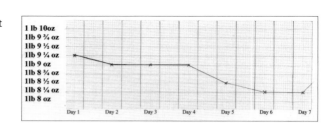

In addition to a written record, I also like beginners to use a visual record or graph, which shows very easily how your bird's food intake affects its weight.

6.13 Transport box

Once your bird is trained, you will want to hunt it as often as possible, and this may require you covering some distance by car to fly on good land, with plenty of quarry. If a bird is going to damage feathers anywhere, it will damage them in its travel box.

As well as keeping your bird quiet and contented, your travel box serves a variety of purposes.

- It contains all mute, keeping your vehicle clean.
- It gives you secure, overnight accommodation when away from home.
- It allows you a warm, contained space in particularly bad weather.

Select a dry-cured pair of wings.

Place them back to back and separate at primary/secondry division in wings.

Place a piece of thick string in a figure eight through the wings.

Draw tight and tie in a reaf knot at the base edge (the bit of wing that once joined the bird).

Then tie any food reward onto the lure with a reaf knot.

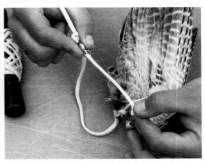

Slide on the swivel of the lure line.

Tie on with yet another reaf knot.

Cut off any excess string.

One finished wing lure ready for use.

In this day and age, all these risks have been taken out of feeding, as many specialist hawk food suppliers now not only guarantee their food, but also give you technical breakdowns of the food's nutritional content, since these food items are produced specifically for the hawk food industry.

7.1 Staple diet

The main food supplied for falconry is the "day-old chicken or turkey chick," which may be purchased frozen in boxes by weight. These offer a base diet to any raptor in much the same way as mashed potatoes will keep humans alive for limited periods. However, on a long-term basis, you will require the supplement of vitamin and mineral additives, if a healthy diet is to be achieved. Day-old chicks are a particularly valuable source of absorbent calcium and are a much-valued part of the young hawk's diet.

Chicks do, however, require some preparation before they can be fed. These young chicks contain a yolk sac, which is absorbed over the first few days of life and is highly nutritious to them. In hawk food terms, it represents a source of hydration, nutrition and colouring for feet and cere.

The yolk sac, however, does have its downsides. In addition to being a possible source of salmonella bacteria, it tends to burst and create a mess in a bird's accommodation or on the glove. It also messes up your bird's plumage. Further, its richness also means it's an incredibly high source of cholesterol, which may be undesirable especially during periods of moult or convalescence when your bird's exercise is reduced.

I prefer to de-yolk my chicks for the most part, feeding them intact only to moulting birds on occasion. De-yolking can be accomplished by removing the feathers around the base of the abdomen, and pinching and pulling the yolk sac out, which when done correctly comes out in one piece rather than bursting.

Quail is also a source of high pro-

A defrosted day-old chick,
prepared and ready to feed.

tein, which is especially good for more active birds like falcons and true hawks. The quail feathers, however, can create quite a mess, so I normally remove feet, wings, head (including crop) and guts, leaving only a small amount of feathers, which aid in the formation of a healthy casting.

Rabbits, rats and mice are also all superb food items high in trace elements, but they are not all suitable for all birds. Falcons, for example, will not do well if fed solely on rabbit, as it is very low in nutritional value and they cannot derive enough nutrition from such a bland food. But hawks benefit from being fed on rabbit, as the larger portions allow their digestive system to operate at maximum rate.

Once you are training your bird, you will be able to experiment with different food types to see how they affect your bird's weight. A Harris hawk, for example, may maintain its body weight on five ounces (142 g) of rabbit just as well as two ounces (57 g) of duck.

Pigeon is actually one of the best meats that you can feed your bird. Although very rich, it is the staple wild diet of many raptors. Great care must be exercised when sourcing pigeon as many carry various diseases that may be transferred to your captive raptor.

The only types of meat I do not feed are mutton, as it gives certain birds diarrhoea, and pork, as its salt content can be very damaging. Wild birds will often scavenge from the carcasses of dead pigs and sheep, but birds in captivity don't have to.

It is legal to use live bagged quarry in the United States for training purposes. So it is important to remember that many game birds intensively reared will carry all kinds of nasty illness; careful scrutiny must be made if considering their use. The use of live food for any purpose is strictly illegal in the United Kingdom.

7.2 Checking for disease and contaminants

From rabbits to mice to pigeons, you should ensure the food you feed your bird is free from disease or contaminants. For example, you must never feed mice or rats trapped around domestic properties because they may contain some elements of poison.

When feeding prey you have caught yourself, it is important to skin the carcass and check for any lead or signs of disease. If you have any doubts, throw it away; it only takes one bad food item to kill a bird! Remember, birds of prey are nature's trash collectors, catching the old, young, weak or sick.

After skinning a rabbit once, I discovered that it was carrying four air rifle pellets just under its skin. I was surprised because when this particular rabbit was bolted by ferrets, it ran normally for more than 200 yards (182 m) before it was caught.

Pheasant and duck are the biggest dangers since they are sought-after game birds and many are shot or peppered, yet they still may live for several years!

Pigeons are particularly prone to diseases, which may be transferred to your bird by ingestion. Wild-trapped pigeon or feral pigeon will normally carry all kinds of diseases such as avian herpes virus and chlamidia (psittacosis), which kills many raptors. Domestic pigeons may carry frounce (a form of avian syphilis), which may be apparent in their mouths in the form of a grey or yellow substance. If in any doubt, freeze your pigeons, as the freezing process will kill the frounce.

7.3 Nutritional extras

If you think your bird's not getting enough nutrition, there are various specialist raptor nutritional products on the market that can be sprinkled over food to add additional vitamin/mineral requirements your bird needs in its captive diet. (See Contacts of Interest.)

Personally, I introduce a small amount of natural oil into my birds' diet in the form of cod liver oil. A couple of drops on food once a week causes no harm and must benefit them if only in production of their own preening oil.

7.4 Castings and crops

Eating some feathers or fur with their meal can help birds produce a "casting," a torpedo-shaped object birds cough up after a meal has been processed. Birds do not waste time separating feathers and fur from bone or meat. They break their meals down into swallowable-sized chunks, which are then passed into the crop (with the excep-

Good and bad casts.

tion of owls, who do not have a crop). The "crop" is a storage bag next to the throat, where large quantities of food can be placed. The food in the crop is easily visible after a bird has eaten.

Casting is very important to your bird's well being as it performs an important function. Meat that sits in the crop for any amount of time gives off fat, which settles in the base of the crop. Over a prolonged period, these fats build up, eventually compromising the effectiveness of the crop. The feathers or fur ingested during a meal act in many ways like a sponge, soaking up these fats, which are then coughed back up by the bird, leaving it with a clean crop ready for the next meal.

Birds of prey will often swallow small stones, or rangle as falconers call it, which are destined for very much the same purpose—to collect fat that when coughed back up clears the crop of pollutants.

Other than owls, most bird of prey species are able to digest even the bones of their prey, so when your bird casts, don't expect to find much more than the feather or fur roughage of the meal it has eaten. A healthy cast should be moist but firm; soft or sloppy casts may be the result of overactive bacteria in the crop. So an eye should be kept on the condition of birds with soft casts.

Every bird is different and the time it takes it to process a crop of food differs, but a bird should cast roughage at least every twenty-four hours. It is important to look for you bird's cast every day, since failing to cast will definitely affect your bird's performance and appetite, and will obviously affect your bird's weight (some large casts may weigh more than two ounces (57 g)). Birds in very low condition may also digest the cast material, resulting in no casting.

If you intend to keep your bird hooded for any amount of time, it pays to skin your food, as a bird will be unable to cast properly in the hood, which may lead in very extreme circumstance to choking.

Alternatively, use hoods with the mouth line out back so the bird can cast with a hood on.

PART 3

SELECTING A BIRD

from these birds, resulting in them flying at very high weights, closely resembling the performance of the wild counterpart.

Socially imprinted Harris hawks can be a pleasure to fly, flying as they do at very high weights. They are also able, in my opinion, to outperform most other Harris's in the hunting field. However, as they require a lot more psychology training, they are best left to the Austringer (flyers of hawks) with much more experience.

8.2 Crèche-reared or co-hort reared hawks

This technique requires baby hawks to be placed in a group or "crèche" aviary on an artificial nest platform. They are given a constant supply of ground food and feed themselves from a very early age. Because they are in the company of other hawks, they grow to realise that they are a bird and not a human. They are in contact with humans, too, when their food bowl is changed, but provided the food bowl is changed without association, they do not see us as parents.

On the good side, these birds are very easy to humanise; they have already accepted human association and very quickly take to our company. They also will fly at very high weights and therefore perform well in the hunting field.

However, these birds may become very noisy or aggressive if dropped too quickly in weight (see Chapter 10: Manning). They are also always very bad at personal hygiene (i.e., preening, etc.). There are two reasons for this: first, they have not had the guidance in hygiene from their parents, and, second, their handlers try to minimise disturbance by not cleaning the crèche too often. As such, the handlers don't keep the crèche as clean as they might.

8.3 Parent-reared hawks

Parent rearing obviously means that the parent birds rear their young from day one. The young birds, flooded with parental care, grow up knowing who mummy and daddy are, learn things like social interaction and hygiene, and have a healthy fear of humans.

People do not realise, though, that even parent-reared hawks may become noisy for a number of reasons. They are incredibly intelligent and quickly make a close association between humans and food. These young birds need to be dropped quickly in weight to prompt a response in training, but then pushed back up in weight to avoid the potential of making noise. If you drop a young parent-reared hawk down in weight too fast during its initial training, the sight of another mature hawk will prompt the bird to start calling, effectively begging to the older mature hawk for food.

Note that some breeders go to great lengths to prevent their Harris hawks from making any sort of noise, even leaving their young birds in an aviary for more than six months. This may stop their birds from making any noise, but it also can make them mentally incapacitated, seeing nothing and nobody. Then, when they eventually start their training, all of the game around them has advanced to the point where entering them can be very difficult.

Red-tails, being slightly less intelligent than their cousins, are slower to make the association between humans and food. As a result, noise isn't a common problem in parent-reared captive-bred red-tails.

Roger Upton carrying a cadge of hunting falcons into the grouse moors in Scotland.
Photo: Terry Spring

Chapter 9

Choosing and Bringing Your Bird Home

Upon your arrival at the breeders, make certain that the birds you have come to choose from conform to your breeding requirements, i.e., are they parent-reared? But, before choosing a bird from that particular breeder, also ensure the breeder has fed them on a varied diet allowing for correct bone and physical development, and kept them in clean, sanitary conditions. If so, the only decisions left are aesthetic.

9.1 Diet reared on

Early-stage development of young birds of prey is governed by diet. Between two to four weeks, they have a very high absorbency of calcium and it is at this stage that the better qualities of food, such as chicks, quail, pigeon, duck and pheasant, should have been fed. Rats and mice, which are also very good for trace minerals, vitamins, absorbed calcium, should also feature prominently in their diet at this stage. If you're happy with the breeder's answers to your diet questions, you can then look at some of the bird's other traits.

9.2 Condition of the bird

The overall condition of the young bird is very important. Are the parent and young birds clean and tidy? Do the youngsters have any traces of mute on their tails (the alkaline content of which over a prolonged period will actually rot the feathers)? Are their feet and ceres soft and shiny, or are they really dirty or dry? Then, on closer inspection, do they have any marks on their feet, which could lead to gross infection? Do they fly freely and confidently within their surroundings? Finally, are they feather perfect, with their full compliment of "hard down" feathers (fully developed feathers with no signs of blood in them)? If your answer to all of these questions is positive, then it's just a case of selecting the bird that takes your fancy, perhaps by its size or sex.

9.3 Size and sex

Personally, size and sex of the species are unimportant to me. The largest bag of game I ever caught in a single day was with the smallest male Harris I have ever trained.

Male Harris hawks are slightly more "birdy," preferring to take on winged species. They also need a little more confidence building when it comes to the initial stages of hunting rabbit, but done properly they can become as proficient as the females (see "Evolution of Male Versus Female Hawks" in Chapter 4: Selection of Species).

Most breeders will try to tell you that they have very large "Superior" or "Sonoran" Harris hawks (larger subspecies from the Sonoran deserts of south-western United States), believing that these are better and more desirable. In my experience, true, pure Sonoran Harris hawks are few and far between. If you can find them, they are seldom better in the hands of a falconer than their smaller cousins, which are also lighter to carry on a full day's hawking. The smaller birds also tend to be faster and more manoeuvrable when hunting avian game species like duck and pheasant.

If you are a complete novice, the female Harris will offer you a slightly higher margin for error when you start to control flying weight.

I normally look beyond size and sex and go for the most aggressive youngster, the one that opens its wings and beak in warning; I find that sometimes this boldness can pay dividends in the hunting field.

The correct position for hands in the casting cloth. / The correct way to cast your bird before hooding. Note that the legs are held firmly, one in each hand whilst the cloth holds the bird's wings together to avoid a struggle.

9.4 Catching up

Once your bird is chosen, I would advise you to allow the breeder to catch it, as the onus will be on him or her not to damage or unduly upset the other youngsters. Most breeders will use a soft net, which is what I prefer. It's quicker and less stressful than chasing them around the aviary.

Once caught, take the youngster around the legs and wrap it (cast) it in a soft cloth or towel. I personally like to manhandle or cast my birds as little as possible. The very fact that you have caught them up in their aviary causes enough stress without sticking them in a box and then going through the whole procedure again when you get home!

9.5 Try on equipment

Hopefully you have taken along to the breeder's a selection of likely sized hoods, as well as the jesses, bells, bewitts and tail-mounts you made, and the tools to fit them. At this stage, you should have your equipment or furniture ready to fit.

Whilst the bird is cast, you can try on your hoods and select the best one for fit and comfort. The best way to check this is to fasten

The selection of furniture you should have ready—bewitt and bell, eyelets and tool, swivel and leash, mews jess and flying straps and tail bell equipment

the hood braces (making sure that it's not too tight!) and then try to remove it by gently pulling on the hood plume. If it slips off easily (when the braces are fastened), it is too large. Check around the beak opening and ensure it is not rubbing on the cere and beak sides, but it is a light-tight fit. Here's a little tip—wet around the inside of the beak opening of the best-fitting hood. When replaced it will start to dry to the exact contour of your bird, ensuring a perfect fit!

As long you hold the bird firmly and correctly, take it indoors (in case it should slip loose) and start to fit the rest of your equipment. Ask the breeder or a friend to sit down and take the hooded

Marking the correct size of bracelet on the bird.

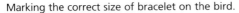

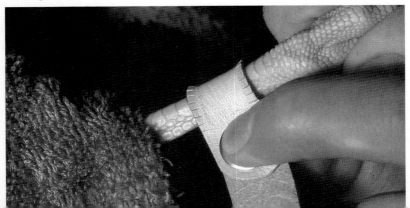

bird from you, placing it face up, onto their knees. Make sure they don't apply too much pressure around its back, as this is where the birds air-sacks are situated, and it is possible to affect its breathing by holding it too hard. If your bird is correctly cast, you shouldn't even need to hold its back or wings, as the cloth will hold them firm to its body and restrict its struggle.

Start off by fitting your bracelets. You will already have the strip of leather for your bracelet cut. One end will already have a hole made and one half of the brass eyelet will have been inserted.

With the hole punched for the eyelet and the excess leather trimmed, we are ready to start fastening up the bracelet. With both sides of eyelet in place, insert the closing tool.

Use the closing tool to fasten the bracelet together.

The finished fitted bracelet.

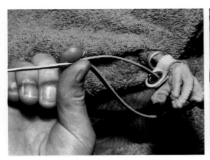

Place the leather strap through the bracelet eye and feed the point through the hole in the strap, pulling it up to attach to the bracelet. / The permanent flying jess is attached.

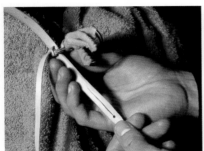
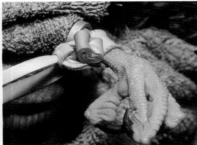

Next, slide your mews jess through the bracelet. / Ensure that both buttons are sited on the outside of each leg (rather than together in the middle).

Once both mews jesses are fitted, start to attach the swivel.

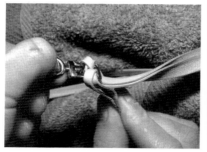

Swivel in place.

Finally, insert the leash.

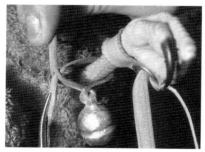

Place the bewitt and bell around the chosen leg, and insert one half into the pre-punched hole, drawing it up (but not too tight).

Using your hole punch, punch a hole in the strap you have just pulled through, and feed the opposite half of the bewitt through it.

Once pulled tight, cut a small arrow-head in this strap to stop it from pulling back out

Cut off any excessive leather, leaving the fitted bewitt in place.

Place this strip of leather around the leg and use the eyelet to make an impression of the place to make your next hole (allow enough room for a little movement and the closing tool).

Once the right place has been established, punch the second eyelet hole and shape with scissors. Fasten it to the leg using the closing tool, making sure any breeders rings are on top of the bracelet nearest the knee.

Next fit your bewitt and bell onto a leg above the bracelet, but below any breeder rings.

Your bird now has all of the leg equipment fitted, so turn it over and place its feet into a cushion, to avoid it puncturing its own feet.

Now, count the tail feathers (it should have twelve) and select the two centre, or "deck," feathers. I like to slide a piece of card into position at this stage and fold around the sides, holding it in position

The leather tabs are fed around the centre tail feathers.

The leather tabs are glued into position.

Slide the plectrum into position.

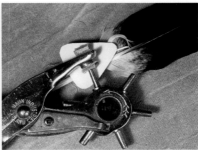

Next, punch a small hole in each tab, as near to the plectrum as possible.

with a few small bulldog clips. This allows you to focus on the centre feathers and prevents any glue or mess from getting on the other feathers.

Glue and place your pieces of tail-mount leather around the feather shafts ensuring that you are fitting it as high as possible, three-quarters of an inch (2 cm) below the point where the feathers enter the body.

Then slide your plectrum over these leather tabs, cut to size, punch a small hole in each and finally pass your cable tie through them to attach your bell.

Pass the cable tie through the holes.

Finally, attach your tail bell and fasten the cable tie, removing any excess.

The tail-mount in use. (Note: telemetry is attached in this photo.)

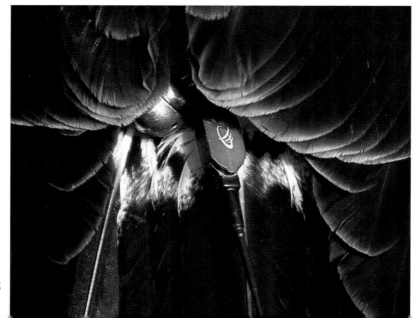

Next, sprinkle a little talcum powder around the site of operation to soak up any excessive glue and stop anything else from sticking together. Unfasten your bulldog clips and slide the card out, leaving you with your fitted tail-mount. This whole operation should be performed as quickly but as thoroughly as possible to avoid the bird overheating.

You are now ready to stand your young, hooded bird on your fist for the first time. Tie the leash onto the tethering ring of your glove and place the jess into the safety position. Allow your colleague to place the bird's feet onto your glove and agree when you're ready for him to let go. It's now time to put yourself in your bird's mind for the very first time: *It's dark, the last thing you remember was being grabbed by a human and held down. Instinct tells you to fly! Get away …*

If it flies off, you are going to need to get your bird back up on the fist. A word of warning—a bird that is hooded can be extremely sensitive to touch, just as you would be in a dark room if somebody started prodding you. Watch that it doesn't grab your hand or fingers because when hooded it may just panic and squeeze, which hurts a lot! On a lighter note, I know of one individual who, for some reason, allowed a young, hooded buzzard to grab him through his trousers in the testicles. He learned very quickly how to handle and touch a hooded bird!

To put it back on the fist, place your hand around its upper breast and lift it gently back into the upright position, placing its open feet onto the correct part of your glove. A bird with closed feet will not stand up. If this is the case, gently rub its feet against your glove to open its feet.

Do not now or ever try to swing your bird back up. A bird is

A freshly equipped young hawk on the fist.

The slit in the tail guard is slid onto the bell and then fastened with the velcro.

not a yo-yo or ball and cup game. This is the reaction of somebody who is clearly not suited to the subtle art of falconry.

The bird may jump off again, but by repeating this process, you will eventually succeed, and your bird will now balance on your fist. Carry your bird around and get it used to balancing on your fist, in preparation for balancing in its travel box on the car journey home. This is not the time to remove the hood, so leave it on and concentrate on allowing the bird to balance.

If you are really well prepared then you will also have a tail guard with you, which will allow you to limit the damage to the young bird's tail feathers, in case it manages to get the hood off on the way home. A bird's tail is a little like a fanned pack of cards; if one should be suddenly pulled out, the rest will collapse. By keeping all of the tail feathers closed, the tail remains stronger.

The next step is to place the bird into your pre-prepared travel box for the journey home. By gently touching the back of its legs against the perch, it should step back. I normally like people to pick up my own captive-bred birds in the early evening as it is normally cooler and stresses the birds out less.

On your arrival home, bring the bird to your bow perch, which you should have already placed in a quiet, secure accommodation. Your bath should not be present at this point of training (see Chapter 5: Housing Your Raptor). Tie your bird down to your bow perch using two (yes, two) falconer's knots. Young birds are more likely to undo their knots sooner than later.

I owned a female Harris that had the uncanny ability to untie falconer's knots in seconds. For fun I timed her one day untying ten knots in a very long leash. It took her just over six minutes! I wonder if Houdini believed in reincarnation?

Some people like to use all manner of fancy dog clips or gadgets to avoid using the falconer's knot. But, in my opinion, falconers have been using this knot for more than 200 years, so why change? Dog clips are heavy, can spring open or break, and can freeze in cold weather.

The best way to tether your bird correctly and safely is to rest your fist on the top of the perch, avoiding the bird's tail. This takes the weight of the bird off your arm and also allows you to gauge accurately the leash length you are giving the bird.

Resting your fist on top of the bow perch allows you to gauge the correct length to tie your bird.

Shorter is kinder—the shorter the leash, the less speed is built up if the bird bates and the less stress is exerted on the bird's legs. Once the knots are tied, gently press the back of the bird's legs (not its feet) against the perch and the hooded bird should step back. If not, carefully lift its largest inside toe out of your glove and guide the foot onto the perch as you lower your fist, feeling the higher perch it should step on (watch your fingers). Once on the bow perch, back away and leave the bird in peace.

For obvious reasons, the area around the perch should allow the bird enough room to bate without any part of its body or wings coming into contact with something that may potentially break feathers. Also the floor should be made of a suitably soft material like grass, fine pea-gravel or even damp sand to prevent damage to feathers or feet when it bates (see Chapter 5: Housing Your Raptor).

Above all, common sense should prevail. Make sure the bird is not in direct sunlight, causing it to overheat, or alternatively in an area where rain can soak it.

So, you have equipped your bird and brought it home, and it is now ready to train.

PART 4

TRAINING YOUR BIRD

Chapter 10

Manning

The first step in training a bird is called manning, which refers to the humanisation of the bird. There are various techniques employed to this end, all of which are meant to achieve the same goal. Some more antiquated techniques involve physically exhausting the bird or starving it into submission. Such techniques are cruel and unnecessary.

Instead, try putting yourself in the bird's position. It has been taken away from its parents or the wild (if in North America), and forced into an alien environment. It has been shackled around the legs and tethered to a perch in complete darkness (due to the hood). Every sound at this stage is intimidating. (Hooding is, however, much kinder for the first few days, because every leaf that blew, every bird that flew over, would terrify it.)

Some people believe that manning involves carrying your bird around on the fist continuously for the first few days. Although carriage does play a part in later training, the first step is to practise "constructive manning," as described by the late Jack Mavrogodato in his book *A Hawk for the Bush*. Constructive manning is a very simple psychology; for the first few days, you only handle the bird when it feeds. It eventually looks on the fist as a place of food, pleasure, comfort and contentment, rather than a place of imprisonment.

10.1 Prepare a room and the food

The first obstacle you will face in manning is to get the bird to accept food from you. As this lesson often takes quite some time, you must prepare a suitable place to conduct it. Many older books on falconry recommend a comfortable chair in a dark room lit only by candlelight. But the reality is that every time the bird flaps its wings, the candle blows out!

Be aware that there is also probably going to be a little mess, be it dripping blood from the food you are feeding or perhaps an errant mute from your bird, both of which may not be welcomed on your spouse's best carpet. I have a room at my facility that is equipped especially for this purpose, but I also have more than 140 birds. Beginners can use any room that will effectively serve this purpose.

In the room, you will need a chair that allows you enough height to keep the bird clear of the ground should it bate from your fist. It should be located in such a position to allow the bird full wing clearance from any obstacles. Dim the background light so it is not startling bright, but light enough to allow the bird to see food on the fist. If the room has windows, draw the curtains so the bird has no other focal point to worry about. Also, ensure there will be no disturbance from third parties. Some people put down sheets of newspaper to catch any potential mess, but be warned that if the bird flaps, the newspaper may blow, frightening the bird even more.

The final bit of preparation is food for the bird, which experience has taught me is the most important thing to prepare. As you will be keeping your bird hooded for long periods over the next few days, ensure that you take any casting material from your food. Prepare food that you know the bird has eaten before and ensure it's easy to eat. If you are going to use something like the leg of a rabbit, pre-slash it with a knife so that the meat comes away easier as the bird pulls at it.

A young, male Harris hawk that just finished its first meal on the fist. (Note the subtle back light.)

10.2 Pick up and weigh your bird

Before you begin this very first lesson, weigh your bird, which will provide essential information throughout the training. Pick up your bird by approaching quietly, placing the back of your glove gently against the back of the bird's legs and applying a little pressure. The bird should step back onto your glove. See the following photographs to see how to pick your bird up for the very first time.

If it does not step back onto the glove, but rather is startled and jumps away, use what I describe as the scoop method of picking up—place your gloved finger and thumb around the leash and run them up to the jess and swivel, lifting the bird clear of the ground as you do so. Place the swivel in the safety position (between middle fingers) and close your gloved fist. If the bird isn't already in the

Bird tethered to a bow perch hooded, but listening. / Approach the bird quietly, and touch the back of the bird's legs with your gloved hand to encourage it to step backwards. If it does not, apply a little pressure to the back of the legs (not the feet).

The bird should step back up onto the glove.

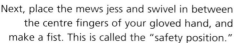

Next, place the mews jess and swivel in between the centre fingers of your gloved hand, and make a fist. This is called the "safety position."

upright position, sitting on your glove, lift the bird back onto the glove and, if necessary, move your gloved hand under its feet until instinct tells it to grab what it feels. (Note: watch any unprotected fingers at this stage!)

Once on your glove, the bird (even though it is hooded) will always wish to stay at the highest point, a little like a person standing on a barrel in a river. If the barrel rolls one way, the person must roll the other; if it goes up at one end, he or she must step to that end to keep out of the water. Keep your fist slightly higher than your elbow, with wrist bent back slightly, allowing your bird a broad, comfortable perch.

At this stage don't just drag the swivel through your bird's feet and into your hand. Roll your hand slowly backwards to get the bird to step away from your finger and thumb. Once clear, place the jess and swivel between your first finger and thumb, and into the palm of your hand. Then slip the

Finally, keeping your fist still and level, resting on the perch, untie the bird's leash from the perch, re-tie it to your glove before gently moving up and away from the perch.

swivel between your middle finger into the safety position. Roll your fist slowly back into a comfortable position for both you and the bird. You can then rest your fist on the perch whilst you untie and retie the bird onto your glove.

Once tethered, stand slowly and make your way to your weighing room. Never weigh your hooded bird without tethering it to your glove. It may at some point in the future fly off (even when hooded) and hit an obstacle at great speed, resulting in injury or death.

Avoiding your bird's tail, touch the back of the bird's legs against the scale perch and encourage the bird to step back onto the scales. It is unusual for a bird to bate in the hood, but be ready just in case. You should always try to weigh the same amount of leash rather than trying to lift the weight of the swivel and leash.

If you are using balance scales, put an approximate amount of weights already on the counterbalance pad so you can simply add or take away weights. When weighing birds, people often say to me that their bird is so many pounds and ounces, including the weight of jess, swivel and hood. If you always weigh the bird wearing this equipment (as you should), the equipment will always weigh about the same, so don't worry about the weight of equipment at this stage. Just say the bird weighs so many pounds and ounces (weight can be critical right down to 1/16 of an ounce (1.8 g) in smaller species). Make a note of its weight using your weight chart (some people like pounds and ounces, others grammes).

10.3 Unhooded on the fist

Then pick the bird back off the scales by touching the back of the legs with your glove, gentle lifting its tail clear with the other. Take up position, sitting with no disturbance, hooded bird on fist and food ready.

If you intend to work your bird with a dog, it is at this very first stage of training that they must be introduced, but in a very controlled environment. If your dog is quiet and well behaved, get it to sit and stay maybe five feet (1.5 m) away from you and your bird in full view, throughout the initial training sessions. If it is a little more jumpy or active, then perhaps a travel cage can be employed in the room to ensure that your dog doesn't upset the young hawk.

Making sure that the swivel is in the safety position, place one of the hood braces in your teeth, take hold of the other and firmly pull them apart in one quick movement. Then leave the unstuck hood on the bird's head.

Try to get into the habit of counting to ten before removing the hood, as your bird will eventually start to realise that as soon as you touch the braces the hood will be coming off, and often starts to move its head around in anticipation of this. By leaving it on for a little while, the bird realises that although it may be undone, it is not coming off right away, making undoing the hood easier in the long term.

Quickly and quietly, remove the hood and place it where it can be easily retrieved. Now it's time to think like your bird again: *You are suddenly cast into light (although it's fairly dim); you are sat on a human hand, should you try to get away? Quick fly away! Why aren't I going anywhere? What are these things around my legs?*

It is extremely unusual for a bird at this stage of training to swing up onto your fist and regain its perch; it will normally just dangle by its jess under the glove. Keeping your jess short (without actually pulling the young bird's legs together), place your hands gently around the upper part of your bird's breast (preventing its feet from grabbing you) and place its feet onto your glove.

It is unlikely for a young bird to physically stand up on the fist if its feet are closed and knotted, so try to make sure that its feet are open as you place it onto your glove. You can do this by moving your glove against its feet, again creating an annoyance that it may strike out at. Remember, do not try to flick it back up onto your fist or try to lift the bird up by its back. Experience will teach you that birds hate to be touched on their backs (it's their one vulnerable point) and they will tend to jump away from the physical threat of your hand. It may take a couple of attempts before the bird stays upright.

Once upright, use common sense. The act of looking someone directly in the eye is an act of aggression. This is the case with most animal species—think about the wolf in the wild. The submissive posture is one with no eye contact, looking at the ground, remaining perfectly still. Hopefully the bird will be a little bit shocked and at best will sit glaring at you. At worst, it will be repeatedly bating off the fist.

10.4 Feed the bird

Once sitting on the fist, try to draw its attention towards the food. This can be done by moving the food in your fingers slightly and animating the meal. Remember, birds of prey are stimulated by movement. After a while your bird may decide (if hungry enough) to bend down and start to pull at the meal. If prepared properly, it should be able to pull off a lump with very little effort, the taste buds kick in, and instinct tells it to swallow.

If it hasn't attempted to feed after, say, one hour, you may need to be a little more proactive. Moving slowly and deliberately, break a small piece off and offer it to the bird. It may jump away from you, bite or try to foot you (strike out with its feet). Or it may just take the food.

One of my favourite tricks with stubborn birds is to break off a long thin piece of food and dangle it (as the mother does to the baby)

Ensure slow passive movement during the first lesson.

just in front of it. I believe that something stirs in the bird's memory, perhaps the memory of its first few instinctive meals taken from its mother's beak.

Let's say that the bird is a little more nervous and won't even sit on the fist. Try to get it to sit unhooded on the fist in a totally dark room, then localise the light around your fist and the food by using a narrow-beamed torch. Once the bird starts to feed gradually, increase the amount of light in the room. It may take up to three hours a day for two or three days to get your bird to feed on the fist, so be patient. As a last resort, you may want to try leaving it unhooded on its perch with food present, then hide and wait for it to feed. Before it has eaten its fill, get in and pick it up using the scoop method, as described earlier, take it indoors and try again. The act of actually feeding stimulated the taste buds and saliva glands, which probably made the bird realise just how hungry it really was.

Your young bird will have been well fed by its parents and will have fat reserves on which it can survive for a number of days. Birds do not ever die from malnutrition, but can die from dehydration. Your bird might be okay for three to four days without food, but watch for dehydration in warm weather. Danger signs of this include shrivelled cere, sunken eyes or saggy, baggy skin on the feet. If you feel that your bird is becoming dehydrated, remove its jess, swivel and leash, and release it in its chamber to feed liberally for a couple of days. There is no disgrace in starting again after a couple of days. Better to lose three or four training days than wind up with a dead bird.

Let's now imagine that your bird is tucking into the meal on your fist heartily. I normally like my birds to take two to three ounces (55–85 g) of food at this stage (remember no casting). When feeding, let it be; don't try to help or pet it. You may, however, want to start making some forms of passive movement, such as lifting your right arm slowly or moving a leg occasionally to initiate movement in its presence.

Red-tails differ slightly in their training here. They will often misinterpret your moves around them, thinking that you are either going to steal their food or offer them more. Both of these interpretations can lead to them footing you, which of course should be avoided at all cost. Make sure that all the moves you make around a red-tail are slow and deliberate. Above all else, never offer them food from your bare hand. Make sure they take all their food by pulling it from your glove. If possible, try not to allow them to see you putting food into your glove at this stage, which can be done by careful employment of the hood.

Towards the end of your Harris hawk's meal or when your red-tail has completely finished eating, start to touch its feet, then stroke the lower breast using the back of your hood. You are going to hood it now anyway, so try to get it to accept the hood in close proximity. What better time to achieve this than when the bird is absorbed in eating? In an ideal world, you would want to hood the bird before it finishes feeding, before it gets the chance to bate (see discussion of hooding in Chapter 6: Equipment).

10.5 Repeat the process

Once hooded, repeat the weighing and work out by subtraction how much your bird has consumed. Write it down on your weight chart. Replace your bird back on its weathering perch hooded and leave it undisturbed for twenty-four hours. Check it regularly to ensure it's fine. When twenty-four hours have passed, it's time to repeat this whole process. Your objective over the next couple of days is to do nothing other than getting your bird to feed confidently on your fist, and if the bird does bate, it should now be able to get itself back up on the fist. And you will through thought and common sense start to understand why it bated, and try to avoid that situation or work towards overcoming that fear through manning.

10.6 Move on with training

Once you have achieved confident feeding from the fist, it's time to move on with the training programme. Weigh your bird daily, trying to keep its weight constant. Monitor the amount of food it consumes. If you find that it is not readily feeding, then give it a smaller ration of food one day, which will give it a slightly lower weight, but it will be hungrier the next day.

You will now attempt to start moving whilst the bird feeds. Try to stand and walk around the room when it is occupied with its meal. Remember that at any point you can end the lesson by hooding your bird. Gradually you are now trying to expose your feeding bird to more and more new sights and sounds. Maybe it's time to meet your partner and kids, open the curtains or feed outside in direct sunlight.

In these early stages, your bird will have good all-round vision; the only place it cannot see is directly behind it. With this knowledge you can make sure there are no sudden surprises from directly behind the bird, which may undo all of your hard work.

This is the time to start prolonging the manning sessions by giving the bird tougher pieces of food that take longer to consume. These are called tirings. The backbone of a rabbit, the neck of a goose or the front leg of a deer are all very good tirings to use at this time. As time progresses, your bird should start to become very relaxed on the fist and the food can be removed for short periods of time.

10.7 Pick up the unhooded bird

Now it's time to work towards the goal of picking your bird up unhooded. Up to this point, you have been replacing your hooded bird on the weathering perch until the next lesson time. Now you are going to work towards allowing the bird to be perched out unhooded.

At the start of the next lesson, unhood your bird and start to feed as normal, using a small amount of food on the glove. Once this is finished, try backing your bird gently onto the back of a chair or elevated perch. Keep the leash securely tied onto your glove and step just out of the bird's reach. Place more food back on the glove and move it suggestively on the fist, whistling at the same time. If the bird is relaxed enough in the environment, and if he is hungry enough, he should step or jump the short distance to the food and also begin to associate your whistle with food.

You now must set the following rule, which must be observed throughout the life of the bird: whatever food you have on your fist belongs to your bird and should never be taken away from it. Never take food away or pull food from your fist. This will only make your

Young Harris hawk being encouraged to jump the short leash length to the glove.

Chapter 11

Carriage

You now have a bird that sits on your fist in a controlled environment, accepts food from you, is able to sit outside unhooded, but that jumps to you for food to start every lesson. Well done!

You now need to work on getting your bird used to the daily sights and sounds it will come across in its life as a falconry bird. Rather than just sitting or walking around in a room or standing outside, you need to get your bird used to things like traffic, farm animals, strangers, and even aircraft and balloons. This period is called carriage because that is essentially what you will be doing—carrying your bird around.

During carriage, the bird is more interested in the food than its surroundings.

11.1 Teach while feeding

Only start these lessons when you intend to feed your bird. For example, say that you wish to get your bird used to traffic. Carry your hooded bird to a safe position, say 100 yards (91 m), from a busy road. Place the food on the fist, unfasten the braces, wait ten seconds and remove the hood. Draw your bird's attention to the food, and it should start to eat.

Slowly walk nearer the road until the bird starts to show signs of nerves, such as stopping eating or getting tight feathered, ready to jump off your fist. Stop and encourage it to take more food. Gradually resume walking until you are ten feet (3 m) from the road.

Standing with your back to the oncoming traffic serves two purposes. First, it gives the bird full view of the cars as they pass, rather than seeing them whizz past from behind in its blind spot. Second, it shields the bird from the drivers' attention, avoiding accidents.

Once your bird is used to this environment, introduce it to other potentially scary situations that you think it may eventually come into contact with while hunting.

11.2 Jumping from objects

All the while you are doing this, encourage the bird to step or jump up to you from different objects. Some falconers believe that by doing this you are rewarding your bird for sitting on these objects, when in fact the bird really doesn't care what it has sat on. The real lesson here is that it will jump to you for food in any situation.

Remember, always step the bird backwards onto these objects. Never let it jump onto them as it will start to anticipate where you want it to go and bate off at every elevated object you pass.

This whole period of training can take anywhere from ten days to two months, depending on both your bird and yourself. After, you should have a bird that is unhooded on its perch most of the time; a bird to which you may now offer a fresh bath each morning; a bird that jumps to you as you pick it up if you offer food; and a bird that is relaxed out of the hood in just about any situation. So it's time to move on to the next stage of training.

Chapter 12

Calling Off

After the manning and carriage stages of training, you can now work towards flying your bird free. While manning your bird, you have been weighing it on a daily basis, monitoring both weight and food intake. This carefully recorded information can now be put to good use.

12.1 Determining flying weight

There is no hard, fast solution to the question of determining flying weight. Just like humans, birds differ in temperament and metabolism. I have birds that were bred in the same year, from the same mother and father and of the same sex, and yet the two individuals started out at flying weights varying almost three ounces (85 g).

If you are training a captive-bred eyeass, then the probability will be that it has started its training from a very fat weight. If this is the case then we can apply a starting rule that will at least get us to a ball-park flying weight.

Allow for a weight drop from day one of the training to say day twenty (or the calling off stage, whichever is sooner) of between 10 to 15 percent. This drop should get you to the approximate flying weight area, but I must stress that this is not always the case especially with birds taken up for training that are older or have real psychological hang ups (long-term parent-reared hawks kept in total solitude). The older the bird, the greater the drop in weight will be required to prompt a response.

The passage bird is a completely different matter. It really depends on the time of year and condition of the bird when it was trapped. In midwinter a passage bird may already be in low condition so very little drop in weight will be required to prompt a response. In late summer, the bird will probably be in better physical condition and therefore a greater weight loss will be required.

A young bird in training will rarely put on too much weight. Being a little nervous it will tend to satisfy its immediate appetite then cease feeding. This normally means that the bird will not eat enough to maintain its body weight over the first week or so.

As training progresses and the bird calms, it will start to feed more confidently and therefore start to take enough food to maintain body weight (sometimes too much), which means that a careful eye needs to be kept on consumption.

A gentle weight drop of certainly no more than one ounce (28 g), but preferably ¼–½ oz. (7–14 g), in any twenty-four-hour period would be recommended, but in the first stages of manning it is not unusual for your bird to suddenly drop an ounce a day until it establishes its daily feeding on the fist routine.

Obviously, weight charts will need to be logged and monitored carefully to stand any chance at all, but there are always danger signs that can be looked out for to stop your bird from becoming too low in condition.

12.1.1 Signs of an underweight bird

Look for the following danger signs of a bird that is underweight:

- It will become particularly desperate on the fist, squeezing hard or almost laying down, with wings mantling the food.
- The eyes may become almond shaped, gradually closing (note that when preening a healthy bird may sometimes partially close its eyes).
- It may sit fluffed up on both legs as if cold in apparently warm weather.

If any of these signs occur, see Chapter 19: Health and First Aid.

Careful use of the weight chart and graph should prevent an underweight bird. But try to work to your speculative weight line, only deviate below this if you feel there is no other alternative.

12.2 Tying a creance line

You need to select several locations for the next training process, ideally fields with short grass. I normally employ an assistant for the next part of the training process, but if you do not have one, you could use a fence post or gate (a lot more entertaining than some of my assistants!).

Pick up your bird as normal, hood it, weigh it and write down its weight. Then carry it to one of your chosen sites and take out your creance line. Fasten it, using two falconer's knots, onto your swivel. Do this without removing your leash, which at this stage should still be fastened to your glove. The reason for leaving the leash on is for safety. What if the bird were to suddenly bate whilst you were tying the creance on?

Once the creance is securely tied, remove the bird's hood and leash (remember the procedure) and give it a small tidbit (betchin) of food. Either back the bird onto the post or encourage it to jump to your friend's fist for food.

12.3 Call off

Walk upwind of your bird and once in position, draw your creance line out to about five feet (1.5 m), wrap it securely around your little finger, face your bird with your left shoulder, extend your arm parallel to your chest and place a one-ounce (28-g) piece of food in your glove, whistling as you do so.

Note that your stance is important. Your young bird if an eyass may as yet be unskilled at flying, having only flown free in the chamber it was reared in. It isn't very good at braking or turning. If you are standing incorrectly, it may accidentally over-fly the fist and hit you. If your fist is in line with your face, the result could be disastrous.

Allowing your bird to fly into the wind is also important. Your bird has a streamlined shape and is designed to face the wind. In flight it slows down by opening its wings and tail, increasing its surface area against the wind. To do this with the wind behind would result in it going even faster.

If your bird does not come immediately, try to animate the food, either by wiggling it in your fingers or by using your bare hand to

Note the correct stance—arm is chest level, left shoulder is facing bird and creance line is held securely around the little finger.

move it on your fist. Animation usually does the trick; a young bird can't resist the natural urge to kill something that it believes to be small and possibly injured.

If your bird flatly refuses to jump, it can only be for one of two reasons. It is either nervous of the surroundings and not sufficiently manned, or it is not hungry enough. But which one is it?

Either go back to manning or carriage, or don't feed it anymore and record its food intake and try it tomorrow at a lower weight. How is the bird's weight compared to your speculative weight line on your graph? Is the bird somewhere near the weight you speculated, or is it well above and not hungry enough?

Assuming that the bird does jump/fly this distance, allow it to eat its reward unhindered. Avoid rushing to grab hold of the swivel and jess, as it will misinterpret this as an act of theft and will either

A young bird flying approximately twenty feet (6 m) in an early lesson.

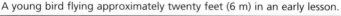

mantle or foot you. Once all the food is gone, show the bird your bare hand and slowly take its jess into the safety position and return the bird to the post/person by backing it on.

You can try calling to your bird again. You will know by studying the bird's weight chart that it requires, say two-and-three-quarter ounces (78 g) of chick to last him the next twenty-four hours. As it has only eaten one ounce (28 g), you can try calling the bird again with more food, but this time doubling the distance. It takes time for your bird's body to process the food in the crop, and a bird with a full crop will still fly keenly until its body starts to feel the food benefit.

Walk out to ten feet (3 m) and repeat the process. Try to avoid rushing any part of this process. Remember that slow, calculating movement is easier for your bird to interpret than fast, erratic movement.

Once the bird has finished feeding again, you can take the equipment back into the safety position and hood the bird. Replace its leash and tie it onto your glove before removing the creance. You will now need to rewind your creance tidily, ready for tomorrow's lesson.

Take your bird home, weigh it and see how much it has consumed. You'll know by its performance whether you feel it was keen enough. If you feel it could have been keener, don't feed it anymore and return it to its bow. If the bird was satisfactory, study your weight chart and top it up with an appropriate amount of food to get it to weight for tomorrow's lesson.

Try at this point to predict your weights very accurately. A drop of more than one ounce (28 g) in a bird of this size over a twenty-four hour period can be harmful. Although your bird may drop in weight like this in the first few days of training, at this stage of training you should be able to balance the bird out, producing a flat level line on your weight graph.

12.4 Increase the distance

Your object over the next few days is to increase the distance your bird flies to you with each flight. For example, if it flies to you ten feet (3 m) today, start at ten feet (3 m) tomorrow and progress to twenty feet (6 m) on the next flight. So each day if your bird progresses, it will go from twenty to forty feet (6–12 m) and from forty to eighty feet (12–24 m), and so on. Eventually, depending on the length of your creance line, your bird should be flying to you without hesitation at least 100 feet (30 m).

Harris hawks, due to their intelligent nature, will get the hang of things very quickly; rather than refusing to come, they will start to take off to you before you even get to your mark. This is a great sign that everything is going well. If you are calling them off from a friend's fist, your friend can turn his or her back on you to prevent the bird from seeing you until you are ready; if you are on your own, this is a little more difficult. When put in this situation, I give the bird a piece of food on its call-off perch to occupy itself whilst I walk to my mark, giving me more time.

Red-tails can be a little slow and lazy at this stage and you need to put in a little more thought to achieve an instant response.

Still, some captive-bred birds will often refuse to fly more than twenty feet (6 m). This is usually due to a lack of confidence that comes from being bred in captivity. Their aviary was probably only twenty feet (6 m) and they have never flown further. You must simply persevere.

Another common problem is they might fly past your fist, snatching at the food as they go by. This is usually the result of insufficient manning; they prefer to steal the food and eat it somewhere more secure.

12.5 The next stage

So, let's assume that any problems have been overcome and you are now at the stage where your bird flies instantly to the fist from 100 feet (30 m) in various locations. You have monitored its weight and have it at a weight to which it responds well. And you realise the amount of food that you need to feed it to bring it back to that weight twenty-four hours later. This is called an initial flying weight.

Whether you have trained just one bird, or are a veteran of many, the next stage in the training process is a big step—the day has come to allow your bird free flight. Many beginners will get to this point in the training and simply not progress, afraid to actually fly their bird free. Indeed, I know of one gentleman who has had his Harris hawk flying every day (even through the moult) on a creance for the past three years!

Before flying free, place your tested telemetry transmitter on the bird's tail. I use a dummy transmitter on their tails the last few days

A young Harris hawk returning to the fist in free flight for the first time.

of creance training to get them used to the weight. Remove its leash and swivel, and leave on only the permanent flying jess. Remove its hood, give it a tiny morsel of food and place it on its normal post and walk away (making sure that you have your spare hand in your bag holding a suitable reward, should it come suddenly).

If your bird hasn't already set off, assume your stance and call it for its normal reward. You'll be surprised at just how much faster it is without swivel and creance, and it should land perfectly. Some young birds, unused to the speed built up over this distance, might overshoot your fist, but they'll normally slam on all the brakes and turn to grab your fist.

Allow your bird to feed unhindered. Don't rush to grab its jess. If it were going to fly away, it would have done so by now! Once finished feeding, gently roll your fist placing its flying jess into the safety position. Repeat this exercise a couple more times before hooding, re-equipping and carrying it back to weigh. Feed it sufficient food to bring it back to its initial flying weight the following day and place it back on its bow perch unhooded to weather (take in the fresh air).

The next day's lesson should be identical, although perhaps in another location, just to make sure your bird is fully relaxed in all surroundings. Your young bird may be a little slower to respond to you from its first tree perch, but have patience; it may simply not know either how to get out or fly from such an elevated position. Time and appetite will eventually resolve any initial problem.

Chapter 13

Following On

Your bird is now flying free, which is a great achievement, but now the real work begins.

In the wild, your bird would have been free flying for the past five weeks or so. It would have had parental guidance and learned many things, like soaring, "thermalling" (to use pockets of warm air to gain height), landing on awkward trees and chasing prey.

You now have to use common sense to teach your captive-bred bird all of these things. I allow my bird to fly free in a couple of different locations to make sure it is keen and responsive. I then begin to encourage it to "follow on," which basically means that I start to teach it how to fly by following me.

The first time in a tree can be daunting to a young bird.

13.1 Initial lesson

Take your bird to a field adjacent to a wood and place it on a post. Walk away normally towards the trees but do not call it. As you get near the trees, if it hasn't already started towards you, raise your glove and whistle. It should set off towards you. Drop your fist, turn your back on it and continue walking. It should fly past you, as there is no apparent reward and land in one of the adjacent trees.

Your bird might, if a little over keen, try to land on your head or shoulder. Don't overreact if it does this. Gently take it on your glove (by offering it at a higher position) without a food reward and take hold of its jess. Try it again, and your bird should get the idea after the second or third try. If it lands on the ground by your feet, approach it quietly and offer it your empty glove as a higher perch to step on. If you give it food for stepping off your head, shoulder or ground, you are effectively rewarding it, indicating that it is doing something right. Your bird should never make this association.

I am not sure if *buteos* are really smart or really stupid, but at this stage they don't develop following on too well. Yet, if you produced bagged game to a passage red-tail, it would be out of the tree and after it in a flash. I feel it is a question of motivation, buteos needing far more than Harris hawks.

Assuming that your bird has flown past you and into a tree, carry on walking past it (into the wind) and recall it to fist once you are approximately 100 yards (91 m) further on. When it comes in, give it a large reward. Some young birds, having landed in their first tree, will panic, not realising how to let go or too scared to jump through the branch they are on. Stay calm and maintain your position; with a little time, they will figure it out and fly to you. If they don't, you'll have to wait until they become hungry enough to come down; appetite is a great motivator!

Assuming all has gone well, you might want to swing your fist forwards gently and encourage your bird into another tree. Carry on walking past its new position and repeat the process. In these early lessons, I never call my birds in more than three times each time for large rewards.

The next day, start off doing the same, but this time carry on walking about 200 yards (182 m). Your young bird should take off to follow without any encouragement at all and, provided you keep your fist down, it should swing up into a tree nearer to you. If this happens, carry on walking and call it in every fourth or fifth time it changes position. If it doesn't follow you, raise your fist as if to call him, then drop it as it gets halfway and turn your back again. It won't be long before it gets the idea.

The object of your next two weeks of training sessions is to try to get your bird to follow you as far as possible each day. Many people forget that appetite initiates training, but repetition completes it. I try to plan a circular route of a distance that I know my bird can manage.

13.2 Initial flying weight

Now you can start to look at your bird's initial flying weight. As your bird starts to develop muscle by following on, it will start to use more energy, therefore requiring more food. To give your bird the opportunity to develop more muscle, increase its weight slowly. Many people make the mistake of increasing the weight higher and higher each day. Ideally, you need to increase weight by one quarter of an ounce (7 g), and then keep it at that for a three- to four-day period, monitoring both responsiveness and performance.

At the end of two weeks, your bird could be flying at anything from one to one-and-a-half ounces (28–43 g) higher than its initial weight. Your bird should now follow you for four to five miles (6–8 km) each day, flying confidently.

If you are flying a passage red-tail, the fitness aspect will have already been achieved through wild flight, so don't worry if you are not achieving your following on goal. Red-tails can be lazy and/or smart, but should be sufficiently fit to move on to the next stage of training.

Young Harris hawk beginning to follow on.

Chapter 14

Entering

Young birds at the "entering" (catching prey) stage of training fall into one of two categories: passive or aggressive. A passive attitude simply means that they show no real interest in natural quarry and they simply will not chase things. An aggressive attitude means that they will chase everything that moves!

It may be that whilst out on your daily exercise walks, your bird has already started to show an interest in the prey birds and mammals of the area. (This will certainly be the case if you are flying a passage bird.) They may have even chased or, better yet, caught something. If this is the case, you can safely skip this chapter, but

Choice of three lures: rabbit, wings or pad.

for most of you training the eyass, your bird may be ignoring prey or chasing it without success.

The normal way of introducing the eyass bird to prey for the first time involves the use of a lure.

Choose the lure wisely as, in the wild, the first prey species caught by a young bird often remains the favourite. Once a young bird associates movement with food, they can often get a little gung ho, chasing literally anything that moves.

One of my very good Harris hawks chased (without success I might add) a lady on a small motorcycle, whom was totally oblivious of her peril. I'm happy to say that my bird grew out of this behaviour and became one of my best hunting hawks.

Many people like the idea of catching large prey with a small bird. I speak to other falconers all the time who tell me about the full-grown brown hares that their Harris hawks catch or the Canadian geese caught with their female red-tail. Some I think are being a little liberal with the truth; it takes a very well-motivated Harris hawk to take brown hares here in the United Kingdom, especially when they are smart enough to know that rabbits are easier and more preferable to catch. In areas where there is nothing else to hunt, your bird, unaware of smaller quarries, will take these larger and more difficult mammals and birds regularly. If you want to specialise at these larger quarries, you must select your "slips" (the quarry at which you release it) carefully to keep your bird oblivious of easier prey.

If you want to hunt rabbits with a male Harris hawk, I would recommend that this is the quarry at which it is flown initially. Allowing confidence to be built on this larger, more difficult quarry will make prey such as pheasants much easier.

14.1 Introduce the lure

So let's say you are going to enter your bird on rabbit. Prepare your rabbit lure (either a dead rabbit or the rabbit lure described in Chapter 6: Equipment), well garnished with a high-quality food reward, equating to your bird's food ration for that day. I present this lure initially to my birds when they are sitting in the weathering yard.

To do this out in the hunting field or at the stage of creance training can be detrimental. If you introduce the rabbit lure to your bird in the early stages of free flight, for example, it may be very frightened of it, spook and fly away, spoiling or at least setting this stage of its training behind. Likewise, to introduce it earlier in creance training may give your young bird the incentive to try to chase prey before it is skilled in flight or fit. The subsequent disappointment will set your bird back in its training.

I introduce the lure after a couple of weeks' free flight and fitness, finding the best place to do this is on the weathering, whilst the bird is tethered to its bow perch. Slide your rabbit lure under your hawk's perch, slowly and quietly making sure that the food reward attached is visible. Obviously, your bird will be tethered to the bow at this point. If your bird doesn't jump straight onto the lure to feed, encourage it to do so by drawing its attention to the food.

Once the bird jumps onto the lure, step back away from your bird to prevent it from feeling the need to mantle. Allow it to feed fully, even if it starts to pluck the lure. Your main objective at this point is for it to feel confident and comfortable with this large furry item.

Once the food is gone, but before your bird has stepped off the lure, approach it. It has no food left and will probably not feel the need to defend the larger lure at this point. Have a small pick-up piece on your glove and encourage the bird to step off the lure and onto your fist. If the bird is holding onto the lure and will not give it up readily, slide your bag over the lure and throw a piece of food out to one side (as far as your bird's tethering length will allow).

Your bird should then jump off the lure and take the food, at which time you should quickly slide the lure into your bag and back away. Your bird now knows that the lure is edible or at the very least has food attached. It has fed confidently and successfully. From this point, you can return to free flying your bird the next day.

Next you need to introduce the lure in a more natural setting. To ensure that the bird has made the bond with the lure, I wait until the end of the following day's exercise and produce the lure whilst the bird is in a tree. I simply pull it out of my bag and pull it slowly behind me. Your bird should remember the previous day's lesson and fly down to feed. Don't worry if it isn't an aggressive attack at this stage. So long as your bird comes down to feed, you'll know that the association has been made.

Young hawk taking a meal from a rabbit carcass.

14.1.1 Getting off the lure

Get into the habit of taking your bird off the lure correctly. Some falconers recommend that you offer your bird a larger pick-up piece held just over the lure, tempting your bird to step off, but this actually creates a running battle with the bird to steal its kill and can also lead to some tail feather damage in the long run.

When taking a young bird off the lure, ensure that the gloved hand holds down the lure, whilst a food reward is thrown out to one side.

I use a different technique, which works very well for me. I stay back until my bird has eaten the food I had tied on. I then approach it and slide my bag over the lure, holding both lure and bag to the spot using my gloved hand. I then throw out a small food reward in front of my bird, just out of reach, to encourage it to jump off. Remember to hold down the lure to ensure that your bird doesn't simply carry the lure with it for this reward. Slipping the lure into my bag, I slide my bag back on and wait for the bird to eat its small reward. I then encourage the bird onto my fist for yet another smaller reward.

If the bird tries to jump forwards off the lure for the food reward but still hangs on, as long as it is focused on getting the smaller reward, you can just unpick the toes that are sticking to release the lure.

14.1.2 Keep practising

Over the next couple of days, increase the speed of the lure. If your bird isn't trying hard enough, don't let it catch it and don't feed it. It's what would happen in the wild!

Next you need to recreate some more natural situations for your dummy bunny to appear from. I use an old mechanical sheep-clipping machine, which has been converted to wind the lure quickly and realistically. I set it up to pull my lure from cover towards a peg away from me.

This young male Harris hawk means business.

133

You can recreate your own scenario, using a long lure line and pegs, or by having a friend produce the lure. Either way, the objective of this exercise is to get your young bird to physically look for game during its daily flights. Produce the lure unexpectedly in different positions in relation to your bird, making it actively alert. Your bird is now nailing the lure hard in various positions, flying strong and looking for game (especially bunnies).

14.2 Dogs

The use of dogs in hunting with birds of prey dates back as far as the sport has existed. I do not profess to be an expert on training dogs, but it's important to know that the introduction of your dog to the hawk should start from the very first day of its training.

Harris hawks more than any other species of bird of prey have an absolute hatred of dogs. This probably stems from the fact that they compete in the wild with coyotes and often fall prey to these larger predators. If you are to stand any chance of creating a harmonious relationship with dog and bird, they must be introduced from day one of training.

There are various breeds suitable to finding or flushing game for your bird, but all will require some degree of training. You do not need a working dog to have success with a hawk in the hunting field, but your game-finding ability will increase as will your overall bag at the end of each season, and you'll have a trained partner ready should you decide to eventually move on to larger falcons.

The commitment of owning and working a dog is as great as that of owning and working a hawk or falcon, requiring even more time for daily training and exercise. But, once trained, their abilities will enhance both your enjoyment of the sport as well as your bird's success rate.

14.2.1 Training your dog

You will need to train whichever breed of dog you choose before you train your bird. This may require you to plan ahead as much as two years to properly train your dog. A badly trained dog will eventually lead to a badly trained or lost bird.

Suffice it to say that your dog must be able to perform basic degrees of obedience before it is introduced to your hawk. It must be able to sit and stay, return to you from any distance when asked, and remain safe and steady with livestock.

Training a working dog throws up a whole new set of questions and problems, which I cannot even begin to answer in this book. If you are convinced that this is the course of action for you, get a good book (see Further Reading), approach the local kennel club and the breed club that represents your particular breed of interest. Try to visit a working test or trial and speak to the owners about the breed's suitability for your purpose. From this you will be made aware of any upcoming litters from which you may secure your new hawking partner. Good luck! You'll need it.

There is no greater rush than when your dog locks up (points).

14.3 Ferrets

The use of working ferrets will dramatically enhance the number of rabbits you will catch with your hawk. Requiring less time and dedication than a dog, ferrets are a much better hunting companion for the beginner. I am amazed that the price of ferrets is so low in the United Kingdom, costing just a few pounds. They can catch dozens of rabbits on a daily basis, providing a freezer full of food for your hawk.

The ferret is a member of the *Mustelid* family like the otter and stoat, developing a very useful, streamlined shape that can be applied to many environments, from water to trees. As you know, the closest relative of the ferret native here in the United Kingdom is the polecat, which is still a wild resident of these shores. In North America, the wild black-footed ferret, although rare, is resident, as is the polecat.

I have read in many falconry books that the only ferrets to use are the white, albino ferrets, which are less likely to be mistaken for a rabbit when they suddenly pop out of a hole. There are in recent times many variants on the natural albino colouration of the ferret, most of which have been derived through careful interbreeding with polecats and their hybrids. I have worked several colours of ferrets with birds and have never had a problem. I have had birds ignore a polecat ferret (brown and black), then seconds later streak off after an ermine (a white stoat in winter colour). Your bird is not stupid; it will eventually distinguish your ferrets from most other prey.

It is important to introduce your bird and ferret correctly and at the right time. I like to keep my ferret run in full view of my young birds right from the first day their hoods come off. By casual association, they gradually become accustomed to them. If doing this, please remember that if you are feeding your ferrets natural food (rabbits, etc.), don't torture your hawk by feeding them in full view.

Some particularly aggressive Harris hawks and most red-tails will try to take and eat your ferrets no matter what you do. Ferrets are very opportunistic predators and would feel equally at ease trying to kill your hawk, so ensure that your ferrets are secure and cannot get close to your unattended tethered hawk.

14.3.1 Training ferrets

Training your ferrets is easy as long as they have a good working background. I start off by handling my young ferrets regularly from the time they reach eight weeks old. They may try to nip but at this age they haven't developed their legendary bite. If my youngsters do nip, I tend to push my knuckles into the back of their mouth, effectively gagging them; they quickly let go. Ensure you handle them confidently and correctly. The correct way to hold a ferret is to place your thumb and index finger around its neck, with its feet between your second fingers. Even if it wants to, it can't physically bite you in this position.

I feed my ferrets as much as they want, trying to give them as much variety as I give to my birds, everything from chicken to rabbit. Some so-called ferret experts recommend that you only feed dry, complete ferret food as it stops them killing their natural prey underground (as they do not realise it is edible). I personally feel that a ferret will only hunt effectively if it is aware that it is hunting a food item.

I start to introduce my ferrets to work when they are around fourteen weeks. I do this by placing them with an older ferret into a rabbit warren that I know has just been "bolted" (vacated). By introducing them in this way, they get the confidence to explore the smells of this subterranean world, without meeting its inhabitants.

A ferret held correctly.

Ferrets have very bad eyesight, so a common mistake is to snatch at them as they come out of a hole, increasing their anxiety. They are already a little nervous about their new surroundings and are naturally on their guard. Old ferreters call this "hole shy," which can be very annoying, wasting valuable hawking time as you try to recover an errant ferret. I like to whistle to them before I pick them up; as silly as it seems, I believe they get used to this ritual and anticipate being picked up. My friend's ferrets will run several feet to him when he shakes his keys (and then they are always rewarded with a tidbit).

Once they start to explore warrens without any sign of nerves, allowing you to pick them from hole entrances without alarm, it's time to get them working. Try a few trial trips out with your young ferret; you may want to take some purse nets with you to catch a few rabbits for hawk food. If using purse nets, use old or weathered ones (hung outside for a couple of weeks) and make sure that you peg them in quietly by hand (no banging). When rabbits bolt, take them and the net away from the hole quickly, kill them in the net (by necking or chopping), and quickly recover the hole with a new net. It's easier to take a dead rabbit out of a net rather than a live one.

My grandfather was a great ferreter and taught me many things about the sport. He had a set of rules that has served me well over the years, which I will share with you.

The rules are as follows:
- Always feed your ferret before work. (A good ferret hunts on instinct rather than starvation.)
- Never ferret between 11:00 a.m. and 4:00 p.m.
- Never get closer than six feet (1.8 m) from a hole entrance. (I introduce my ferrets from downwind; if there is any scent on the hole, they will find it.)
- When a ferret is working, ensure absolute silence.
- Don't ferret when it's windy. (It's far less productive and ferrets tend to kill more underground.)
- Never leave a ferret in the hunting field. (Easier said than done!)

One way to avoid losing your ferret in the hunting field is to purchase a ferret finder from a company called Deben (see Contacts of Interest). The ferret finder consists of two components: a collar with a transmitter that fits around your ferret's neck and a receiver box. When the ferret is working, it is possible to determine where it is (and with experience what it is doing) by the depth and position indicated by your receiver.

If you think that your ferret may have killed, you will be able to dig down to its position and remove both the ferret and the fresh kill from the warren. Obviously, the digging element takes some practice and must be performed with care and caution to avoid injury to your ferret. If the ground is very rocky or very sandy, this option may not be available.

After digging out a ferret, it is important to replace all soil and sods, as wildlife and livestock may break a leg in such a hole, plus a rabbit may then reoccupy the warren if its defences don't appear to be breached.

It may happen that you have to leave your ferret if, say, your ferret finder has stopped working or you can't dig the ferret out in crumbly sand. Note that a ferret in the wild will decimate wildlife and the landowner will not thank you for this.

To avoid losing your ferret, dig grass sods and clog up all and any holes you come across. I like to leave hay from my carry box in one of the larger hole entrances before blocking it. Your ferret's nose will guide it to this familiar smell and you will likely find it asleep on the hay when you return.

One final thought: never force your ferret into a hole it doesn't want to go. He might know something that you don't, perhaps smelling a fox or badger. A good ferret will smell rabbit and be only too keen to go in.

14.3.2 Male or female ferrets

A male ferret is called a Hob, and a female a Jill. The Jill is two-thirds smaller than the Hob. I like Jills because their smaller body size means that they find it harder to hang onto rabbits, getting kicked off rather than killing underground.

If you choose female ferrets, note that they will come into season (oestrus) in the spring of each year. They will remain in season until actual copulation takes place. If this doesn't occur, the risk of

Never try stuffing your ferret into a hole; it may know something you don't.

infection increases. Many people keep a Hobble, a vasectomised male ferret, around to bring your females back out of season without impregnation. (Note that ferret courtship can be a rather rough affair.)

But beware: my friend recently used a supposed Hobble on his three Jills and is now the proud owner of thirty-eight new ferrets. Make sure it really is a Hobble, as it can be difficult to get rid of baby ferrets.

Chapter 15

Your First Hunting Adventure

Your bird is relatively fit, it's chasing and hitting the lure hard and it's looking for an opportunity. You may have even had a few abortive chases. Your bird is ready to start hunting. Pre-planning and even reconnaissance are essential to give your hawk every chance of success. I also find that ferreting is a very good way of entering a young hawk.

15.1 The first chase

Look for a small warren, ideally situated on a slightly sloping, open field. If possible, watch this warren for a couple of days to ensure occupancy. Ideally, the wind should be blowing up the hill. I like to ferret reasonably early in the morning, as the rabbits will still be active and alert from their night feeding, rather than asleep and surprised by the ferret.

Approach the warren silently and place your ferret near the holes

An alert, young Harris hawk, transmitted up and ready for the hunting field.

(downwind) as quietly as possible. Remain alert and ready. Try not to have other distractions in the area. If all goes to plan, your rabbit will bolt and head for either the nearest holes or cover. It can be beneficial to study the rabbit runs in the grass around the area to predict the direction it will bolt.

You are now standing uphill, approximately ten to fifteen feet (3–5 m) from where the rabbit has bolted. If your bird is in optimum condition, in fitness, appetite and motivation, it should set off in hot pursuit, but if it doesn't chase, don't try to throw it off; there will be a reason it hasn't taken off itself.

As the bird gives chase, some falconers do something at this point that has me in stitches of laughter. They shout loud encouragement, perhaps the word "Ho!" What they may not realise is that it is very likely there is another rabbit in this warren, and provided it's oblivious of your presence, you may get another bolt in a couple of minutes, rather than the ferret getting an early lunch.

Once the bird is chasing, its evolution and development will take over from here to determine its success. Some young birds may chase and then suddenly back off. Ask yourself two questions. Is it confident enough in terms of manning and introduction to the lure? Or is it not keen enough? Only you can answer these questions. If your bird will not even leave the fist, again ask yourself these questions.

I find that this is possibly the hardest period of training a Harris hawk. They become friendly and confident quickly, achieving very high weights, but they may not be keen enough to enter at these weights. This is more apparent in males who need to be keen and confident to take on such relatively large prey as rabbits. Passage red-tails, on the other hand, will almost certainly have prior knowledge of this quarry and will normally hunt at the same weight as they free fly.

15.2 After the chase

If the chase hasn't led to a capture, the rabbit may bolt down another hole in the warren. Your bird is sitting, looking down it, and your ferret won't be far behind. Although your hawk might appear to get along with the ferret, the excitement of the situation or indeed the ferret's natural aggression towards any living creature might provoke a disaster. Call your bird back to the fist immediately to avoid this situation.

Let's instead assume that everything has gone well and your young bird has made contact with its quarry. You have a moral obligation to despatch this quarry as quickly as possible and ensure that it does not suffer unduly. Keep in mind, however, that your young, inexperienced hawk may start to have doubts about this kicking, thrashing bungle of fur. So don't go galloping in and frighten your bird off or indeed inspire its prey, faced with yet another terrifying predator, to double its effort and kick your bird off. Run as fast as you can to within ten feet (3 m), and then walk in quietly and take hold of the rabbit in your gloved hand, helping the bird to hold it.

15.2.1 Despatching quarry

When it comes to despatching quarry, there is no substitute for experience. There are several ways in which this can be done, but all must be quick and in no way detrimental to your hawk. I prefer to break the neck of my rabbits using the pull technique. Your bird's legs and feet should be clear of the neck if this is to work. I place my fingers and thumb of my gloved hand around the rabbit's neck and then pull the back legs with my bare hand. Great care should be taken to do this thoroughly, without damaging your bird's feet in your grip.

Another method is to carry a pointed bradawl or screwdriver sharpened to a point, which can be pushed into the rabbit's skull just behind the ears. Try to avoid knives as one slip may result in a serious accident to your bird.

When it comes to killing other quarry, your technique may have to vary. Stoats and weasels, for example, have very sharp, effective teeth, which will cause your bird a lot of damage. I like to push the finger of my glove into their mouths to give them something to bite on whilst I practise the screwdriver method (necking is impossible).

For game birds, necking is best, but if done too hard may result in you pulling their heads off, causing blood to squirt all over you, your bird and everything else in the area. You'll be amazed at the strange looks you will get when stopping at the petrol station on your way home in this condition.

A couple of years ago, a young lady in my employ was giving

Beginner's luck.

some guests a short session flying and handling birds in my flying field. Suddenly, a very out-of-breath guest ran to the mews to tell me that there was a serious problem at the flying field. Without asking what the problem was I ran at full speed to the field. The scene that greeted me was beyond any comedic performance I have yet to see.

One of the Harris hawks had caught a duck (a lucky shot) and my employee had quite correctly made in and dispatched it by breaking its neck. As soon as the neck was broken, the duck's central nervous system kicked in and it started the hangman's jig (meaning that it was in fact dead). So furious was its thrashing that it kicked both the Harris and the lady and proceeded to cartwheel around the park. The young Harris was at a total loss, as was the girl who began chasing the duck around with tears rolling down her face sobbing loudly for help. She now uses an air pistol to despatch all of her kills. (I think she even carries a blindfold but I don't know if it's for her or the quarry.)

A very important lesson can be learned from this story. The act of killing another living thing is not easy. If you are going to be a falconer, you have a moral obligation to despatch your game quickly and efficiently. If there are any doubts in your mind about doing this, don't practise this sport.

A very excited young hawk may mantle its prey at your approach.

15.3 Quarry caught

After despatching the quarry, you should now have one very excited hawk and one very dead rabbit.

Some books suggest that you should now allow your bird to feed, whilst you circle it, approaching every so often with tidbits (to get it used to your approach). Doing this creates its own set of problems. Your close presence at this stage will encourage your bird to mantle, feeling that it needs to defend its kill from you. As I have said before, this can develop into a habit, which can only result in broken or damaged feathers. So step back around twenty feet (6 m) and stay still; avoid looking or staring at your bird, leaving it to get on with the job of feeding.

If you have been training using a natural lure (i.e., a dead rabbit), then your bird will be used to breaking into a carcass. If not, leave it for ten minutes; if your bird doesn't figure it out by then, go back in and open up the carcass to reveal some flesh. I like to let my young birds take a very large crop from their first few kills, even if it means that the bird requires no food the following day.

Once your bird has got a very large crop of fresh rabbit, slide your bag over the kill. Hold down the rabbit and the bag with your gloved hand and encourage your bird to jump forwards for a piece of food. Normally, with a full crop, your bird will just step off the kill, maybe even as you slide the bag over it. Slip the rabbit in your bag and pick up the bird with a small reward.

Try to stick to one kill per outing, rewarding your bird with large crops for the first twenty or so trips, to ensure your bird is confident and well motivated. You will find that with confidence comes an increased body weight and you should be approaching a simulation of your bird's wild weight by mid-season, as long as you are flying daily and your bird is in routine.

15.4 Cleaning up

Once back home, weigh your bird and work out how much food it has consumed. Mark it on your weight chart.

You'll then need to clean your bird's feet and beak, which is a very good habit to get into on a daily basis. I use a mild solution of Virkon and liquid soap in warm water. Use an old, soft toothbrush to work at your bird's feet and legs, paying particular attention to the point where the talons meet the toes.

Harris hawks have particularly long talons, which get wrenched or twisted on impact with quarry. This can lead to an initial mild infection in this cracked or cut area. If left untreated, it quickly

Cleaning a bird's feet with an old toothbrush, Virkon, soap and warm water.

flares up and eventually the toe will swell and become tender to the touch. By keeping these areas clean and disinfected on a daily basis, you will avoid this condition.

Once clean and dry, some people like to rub Preparation H into the feet. This steroid cream was formulated for the treatment of haemorrhoids in humans, as it encourages new skin growth. It can improve the suppleness and colour of your bird's feet, but if there are any open wounds on the feet, the steroid will help to culture the bacteria in the wound. I like to use E45 cream, which although still a steroid, is milder and more specific to dermatology. It will not only aid new skin growth, but if used regularly it also will help to protect the feet, as would a barrier cream.

15.5 Non-flying days

Although it is recommended to exercise your bird daily, there will be days when the weather is too wet, or time does not permit a full session. On these days your bird will still need exercise if it is going to become the athlete you envisage.

15.5.1 High jumping

One technique that people use is "high jumping," which basically means that you encourage your bird to make a series of vertical jumps to your fist, in quick succession. The principle behind it is a little like bench pressing in weightlifting.

I don't personally like this technique much, as I find that it can make your bird overly sensitive towards the glove. It also creates a lot of potential to break feathers and develop bad manners. But you can make up your own mind if it works for you or not. You will need the following equipment:

- Ladder.
- Bow perch.
- Creance line.
- Bag with chopped-up food rations.

Chapter 16

Different Flying Techniques

A variety of techniques can be employed when hunting and flying in different sorts of terrain, provided there is available quarry.

It is important to point out that passage hawks may be reluctant to fly and hunt in terrain alien to the areas in which they hunted in the wild. Attempt to simulate as closely as possible the sorts of terrain you think your passage bird may be used to. You can gradually introduce new environments as your success dictates. Harris hawks are far more versatile and will readily adapt to different environments. This trait allows for experimentation in a variety of terrains at different quarries.

16.1 Waiting on

Waiting-on flights allow your bird to stay on the wing at height for prolonged periods of time and are a great way to build both ability and stamina. Your bird will only adapt to this style of flight if the terrain and quarry are suitable. Try to find quite a steep, wind-facing slope and wait for a windy day. This will only work initially if the wind is blowing directly up the slope face rather than across it. Don't worry if the ground is completely devoid of game; it's actually beneficial in the early stages.

Release your hawk as normal. It might sit on the ground. Walk

Waiting on.

away down the hill and encourage it to follow, as you would do in woodland. If the ground you have selected is good, your bird should start to circle into the wind. Once your bird has achieved reasonable height, about 100 to 300 feet (30–91 m), wait until it is directly above you and call it down for a large reward or produce the good, old reliable rabbit lure. Gradually increase the amount of time on the wing with each session.

Now we need to start thinking about hunting from this position. You will waste your time ferreting when your bird is in this position

With experience, your bird will take to this style of flight, and great things can be achieved!

as the increased interest on the ground scene will encourage your bird to come down and land. Start off by using your lure when the bird is in good position. Make sure the reward is a large one and try to end the session on a high point, for example, at the time the bird has just had a large feed. Try to give your bird some kind of signal that you are about to produce the lure, for example, wave your glove above your head. Over time your bird will start to realise that this signal has some meaning, and will start to position itself above you in anticipation of the flush.

At this time it is very beneficial to make your lure outrun your bird. From a psychological point of view, your bird will feel it needs to be faster, encouraging it to increase its height (pitch). Once your bird is responding to your visual signal, you can now start to effectively hunt wild game.

In this environment, a pointing dog can be very beneficial, allowing you to locate game and bring your bird into exactly the right position before game is flushed. But both dog and bird need to be trained to work together much earlier in the training as discussed.

Beating through groundcover is the next best option. Try to walk over a lot of ground; if nothing else, your bird will benefit from this excellent form of exercise. In this environment, your bird may become much more efficient on winged game, such as pheasant or duck, and produce flights on a par with the true falcons. Experiment with and enjoy your hawk in this situation.

16.2 Woodland hawking

Woodland hawking is one of my favourite ways of hunting. This style of flight, however, should only be attempted once your bird has entered on quarry and is confident. This style of hawking is probably better suited to the Harris hawk than any other species of bird. Red-tails will lend themselves to this form of hawking, but be conscious that they are less agile and slower than the Harris and may not be as successful.

Very dense conifer plantations are impractical places to fly, but more open (not too open) woodland can offer great sport. At certain times of year, the physical plant cover may be six- to seven-feet (1.8- to 2.1-m) high, but in the autumn when this dies down, the groundcover offers excellent protection and sanctuary to all manner of prey species.

There are two requirements to woodland hawk effectively: your bird must be following on well and your telemetry must be accurate. (Make sure you know how to use your telemetry!)

Start by positioning your bird in an elevated position, such as a tree, above the hunting scene. Then slowly start to move through the cover, leaving no area unbeaten. Obviously, you are trying to beat towards your bird's position. Whilst doing this, the objective is not to spot the prey yourself, but to watch your bird.

Your bird's elevated position and superior vision will obviously afford it a greater overview of the hunting scene. Watch your bird's gaze as any sudden changes of view or changes of position or perch will indicate an interest in something. You can now re-angle your attack as beater and try to sandwich the obvious point of interest between you and your bird. Because of the heavy groundcover, you will rarely see the quarry until your bird is upon it. Although the flights are not as visible as in other types of hawking, they are very exciting!

In terms of quarry, I have caught all manner of game in woodland scenarios, from hare to woodcock. Pheasants are a particularly difficult quarry for hawks in the open, as they are far superior in speed, but in woodland scenarios, your success rate will quadruple.

There are, however, two distinct disadvantages to this type of terrain: possibly losing your bird and taking your bird off a kill in cover. Losing your bird in dense cover is a reality, especially when pheasants are present, as they will cover a great deal of ground. Some books advocate the use of good bells, allowing you to locate your bird easier. In my experience, a hawk on a kill in thick cover will freeze at the approach of anybody or anything, perhaps believing that a predator is stalking them. I have had hawks kill in light groundcover ten feet (3 m) from me, and four people could not find it. Clearly, if they do not move, their bells do not ring, so the best bells in the world won't help you. A good telemetry transmitter will, if used properly, get your bird's position every time. Remember that a tail-mounted transmitter will keep the aerial straighter as well as prolong the life of the transmitter.

Taking your bird off a kill in deep cover can present its own set of problems. There are certain positions your bird will get itself into where the normal mode of quarry transfer will not be possible, in a large bush, for example, where your bird may have both legs astride of a limb or branch. If care is not taken in these situations, feather damage or indeed bird damage may occur.

Your first priority as always is to despatch the quarry using whichever method you prefer. Once despatched, allow your bird five minutes to calm down and perhaps start to feed. When the bird has started to feed, try to encourage it to place both legs around the feed area on the carcass, which can be done by partially covering the kill with your bag and then covering the food site with your glove. Your bird, in its anxiousness to keep its prey, will try to hold onto it, moving its legs around the feed zone. Once the bird's legs are free from obstacle, lift the kill, with bird attached, and transfer it to a more open position.

Do not allow your bird to dangle upside down off the kill. Support it until a more open position can be reached. Remove your bird after the normal reward in the normal fashion (see Chapter 15: Your First Hunting Adventure).

16.3 Hawking near water

If hawking around rivers or lakes, there may be a time when your bird kills on water. This is particularly common with water hen flights. Some birds will try to row themselves to shore with prey, but if prey is a large duck paddling in the opposite direction, they are not going to make it. A large stick for wading or testing depth is useful, but there are times when only swimming will do. If this is your last option, remember the best-trained hawk in the world is not

With dog on point, you can determine how far back you want to stand before the flush, increasing the chances for quarries and your sport.

worth your life. Water that looks calm may have a sludgy bottom, sucking you under. Or it may be freezing, resulting in hypothermia, which sets in quickly. If you tend to hawk on the same ground, having an inexpensive, children's inflatable boat deflated and rolled up in a hiding place might mean the difference between a retrieved bird and a dead one.

If the pond is iced over, and your bird has killed on the surface, your creance line stored neatly in your hawking bag can be very useful. Tie one end of the line around a root or branch at water level, carry the line around the pond's edge, returning if possible to your original position at the root. Pull in both sides of this line, effectively hooking your bird's prey and your bird on the line, and pull them off the ice towards you.

16.4 Flying off the fist

When using either dogs or ferrets, it is sometimes possible to predict the position of your quarry before it is flushed. This allows you to position yourself and your hawk in the best possible position, relative to the flush. This will either increase success or, in the later stages of training, purposely make each slip harder for your bird.

Since your bird is evolved to hunt by elevation, you can position yourself as high above the hunting scene as possible, which will give your bird an initial burst of speed thanks to gravity. The wind strength and direction are also important. If you release your bird at quarry running downwind, it will gain ground quickly but have very little control and have to turn in a wider arc than its prey. By flying off the fist, you are able to position your bird as you see fit, hopefully increasing its chances of success in the open.

16.5 Flying in a cast or group

One of the most desirable reasons for flying Harris hawks is to fly them in a "cast" (a pair of birds) or a "group" (a number of birds flying together but not co-operatively). This endearing trait is not present in red-tails; I would urge you not to even contemplate flying more than one red-tail at a time! Whilst it is true that some people manage to fly them in pairs, this is normally only achieved when both are slipped simultaneously at quarry. Having a focal target to concentrate on avoids accidents, but it's only a matter of time before one will happen. Harris hawks are the only bird of prey that can be flown relatively safely together without attempting to kill each other. A group of Harris hawks focused on a bolted rabbit will rarely worry about one another. But they, too, will need to be introduced correctly to achieve this.

If you want to try, make sure that your Harris is properly entered in its own right, having several kills under its belt. Some people make the mistake of trying to introduce a new Harris in a group

A cast of juvenile Harris hawks making a kill.

A cast of well-paired juvenile Harris hawks sharing a kill.

before it is entered, hoping that it will learn from the other birds. Whilst this is true, your young bird will tend to tag along with the flight rather than taking the lead. The result is it entering much later, and becoming more of a problem on the kill.

A well-made (experienced) adult female may relinquish her kill to one of her own offspring, but an unruly, aggressive juvenile may get more than it bargained for should it decide to tangle with this much older, stronger and wiser female.

Once caught, you have to think and act fast to ensure a harmonious relationship between the birds. Get to the kill quickly and work out who caught it. In the early stages, it pays to carry an older kill (rabbit), onto which you can transfer the unsuccessful bird. Hold down the freshly caught rabbit and slip the other rabbit out of your bag next to it. One of the hawks (perhaps both) should transfer both its attention and its feet onto this new prey item. Common sense is required if both transfer; by moving the original kill provocatively, one should change its attention back to the original quarry. In the normal course of events, the bird that actually made the kill will be holding on the tightest anyway, so they normally end up with their own rightful rabbit.

Allow both birds the opportunity to pull on their respective rabbits, but keep a close eye on them. If the older bird manages to break into its carcass quicker than the younger, the youngster may decide it prefers the other rabbit. You'll need to be on hand to sort this problem out. Try, if possible, to allow the birds as much time as possible to feed in full view of each other, but not right next to each other, as this encourages mantling.

When removing them from the kill, try to do it simultaneously with the owner of the other bird. This avoids quarry transference or jealousy. When flying two or more Harris hawks, there will always be one better than the other. If you happen to be the owner of the poorer one, fly it more on its own, increasing both fitness as well as skill level.

In a professional environment, I have had to fly groups of up to twelve Harris hawks together, which requires eyes in the back of your head. I wouldn't ever recommend that you fly in groups of more than three birds. Group flying means that quarry in the area is put under undue pressure and, regardless of its fitness or ability, will fall prey to such large groups, which is not an example of natural selection. In addition, in a group of Harris hawks, a leader or dominant bird will always materialise, keeping the subordinates in order. If your bird is one of these subordinates, its hunting development may be stifled.

If you feel that your bird has worked well with others, you can start to hunt them as a "pack" (a group that hunts co-operatively). Your birds as a team will become a formidable force in the hunting field!

16.6 Lamping

Although the style of flight called "lamping" (catching rabbits at night) may be illegal in the majority of the United States, it's becoming more and more popular in the United Kingdom. If your ground is fairly devoid of quarry, this technique may offer you and your bird more slips and opportunity.

Rabbits are mainly a nocturnal species and far more active at night. If you work during the daytime, this night-time hunting will allow you to fly your bird daily, especially when the early winter evenings move in. Lamping basically involves flying your bird at rabbits at night with the use of a powerful lamp. Your bird will need to be carefully conditioned to achieve this style of flight, but it will certainly increase your bird's head count by the end of the season.

Never attempt to fly more than single birds in this manner, as darkness may result in mistaken identity and then injury. Once your

Lamping rabbits.

bird is flying hard and entered at rabbits, put it back onto a creance line and start to fly it at night, using a small torch to illuminate the food on your fist. Remember that, although the bird may see the food on your fist, it may not see obstacles in its flight path, so try to keep these training areas as clear as possible.

Once your bird is flying in darkness with confidence towards this small beacon of light, you can start thinking about going out into the hunting field. Ideal conditions are moonless nights with a slight breeze, as the wind, if used to your advantage, will muffle both your movement and smell. The best results can be achieved by employing an assistant to work the lamp.

Place pieces of folded cards into the slots of your bells, making them non-audible, and take great care to ensure your telemetry is operational. Use stealth and silence to move into a likely open field, staying downwind, otherwise your scent will be carried to the resident feeding rabbits.

Using a strong lamp (one-million candle power is ideal), allow your friend to quickly scan the field for rabbits. Their eyes should show up red in the lamp. With the lamp off, walk quickly and quietly towards them, using your position to shepherd them away from any close cover, and get within a reasonable range before you flick the lamp back on. Try to walk to your lamp assistant's left-hand side, about twenty feet (6 m) apart. Gauge your bird's reaction to any rabbits that run; if it seems like it wants to chase, let it go!

Keep the lamp on the chase, but be sure to release your bird twenty feet (6 m) from the side of the lamp holder, as its silhouette will obscure the lamp beam, obscuring your bird's view of its prey and spoiling the flight. Your hawk should be able to see any potential obstacles in the more powerful beam of this large lamp, and make any appropriate changes in flight to avoid them.

If the flight is unsuccessful, turn off the large lamp (you may dazzle or blind your bird) and shine your small torch onto your fist/reward (making sure that the flight path to you is clear of any obstacles). The closer you can get to your quarry, the more successful the flights will be. Experiment and you'll have great fun!

But a few final words of warning: your bird, if unsuccessful in pursuit, will probably land on the ground. If the night is bright it may feel insecure in this position and will try to get to an elevated perch, which will cause you to lose it. Some falconers are using chemically activated lights, which can also be employed for fishing floats; these are inexpensive, can be fastened to either tail-mount or jess, and provide a very clear indication of where your bird is located in total darkness. Keep the telemetry handy; you will use it more on this style of flight than any other.

Finally, don't forget that it is illegal in the United Kingdom to hunt any game species other than rabbit with the use of a lamp.

Chapter 17

Tactics for Different Prey

When hunting varying prey species with a Harris hawk or red-tail, it pays to utilise your bird's versatility. I pre-plan the manner in which I try to catch different prey species before I even encounter the species. Here are some of the preferences and styles I have learnt in hunting various species.

17.1 The buried rabbit

By their very nature, rabbits rarely bury on hard, level ground, preferring soft earthy banking. The type of flight you can expect in these circumstances is largely dictated by gravity. If the rabbit runs

A young bunny, alert to danger.

uphill, you are at a disadvantage! If the rabbit runs down a very steep hill, you are also at a disadvantage. You need to plan your attack in light of the terrain.

First, you need an occupied "bury," where a rabbit is in residence, which is relatively easy to find if you have a dog that will mark (show) you such places; harder if you just rely on luck. If you don't have a dog, look at the floor at the entrance to a bury. Is it well marked or padded from use? If you rub your nail or finger against the floor, will it easily mark? If it marks and there are no tracks, you may be sure it is empty. Does it have any fresh vegetation around the hole entrance or is it neatly cropped? Are there any fresh, moist rabbit droppings around? If yes, these are good indicators that the bury is occupied.

Also determine how many holes the bury consists of. Walking very gently, explore the vicinity and try to see any other potential escape routes. If the warren has more than eight holes, I normally dismiss it and move onto a smaller bury.

For the best, sporting flights, I try to plan for my rabbit to flush along level ground to the right and left of the bury. As a result, three factors need to be considered, as follows:

- How far is the nearest bury to which the rabbit can escape?
- Are there any tracks or marks on the ground that indicate the paths the rabbits regularly tread.
- If the rabbit bolted the wrong way, which direction creates the worst-case scenario?

Allowing for these facts, ask yourself whether this setup is ideal for success. If not, move on to another bury. I try to position myself and my bird in the highest possible position that obstructs the worst-case scenario route. My presence hopefully shepherds the rabbit away from this route. If trees are present, encourage your bird to take stand in a position in this area. If you are using a ferret, only allow your bird this type of freedom if both are introduced properly and there are no signs of aggression towards the ferret.

You are then free to act as a further rabbit obstruction. For example, you can walk over to the nearest bury and act as a guard to push the rabbit away from this escape route. If you have friends with you, use them, too, positioning them in any place you don't want the rabbit to run. Make sure that they are very quiet and that they cannot be seen until the rabbit has bolted cleanly from the hole entrance. Bolting flights are great flights for young birds and, if done properly, very successful!

17.2 The sitting rabbit

Flights at sitting rabbit can be very well engineered if a pointing dog is employed. The use of a dog gives you some time to plan the best way to approach the flight. If you haven't got a pointer, you'll require a team of beaters, who, when walking on either side of you in a straight line, will push the rabbit in the direction you are walking.

Study the type of cover and ask if it can be walked through. Which route is going to offer the worst chance of a successful flight? Again if trees or elevated covers are present, utilise them allowing your bird the freedom to use gravity.

17.3 The sitting pheasant

Pheasants are a lot quicker than the average Harris or red-tail, having slightly more acceleration. If they are seen moving in the open, you'll stand little or no chance; it's better to flush them to the nearest cover or woodland.

In cover or woodland, your hawk's chances of success are slightly higher, especially if it has the advantage of elevated trees from which to swoop. If you can mark down (spot) or get a point on a pheasant, you could try the following setup.

Try to position your hawk as quietly as you can in an upwind position of the pheasant. In the highest position possible, flush your pheasant into the wind! If the setup is right, as the pheasant lifts, the hawk will be dropping at

A fine cock pheasant.

A youngster getting the hang of things.

full speed from its lofty position. The pheasant should then try to bank left or right, away from the hawk, which should hopefully bind to it on the turn. Your young hawk will learn the routine if given enough chances, but you will pluck a remarkable number of tails, minus their pheasants, in the beginning.

I used to hunt some ground that was situated at the base of a very steep cliff, below which there was a small rough wood. I would take my Harris to the top of the cliff, throw her off and then run down to work the cover whilst she soared hundreds of feet above. On marking or eventually by pointing a pheasant, I would wave my glove in the air as a signal that I was about to flush. After the first few flushes, she soon got the idea and soared over-head into a strike position. The stoops I got at pheasant on this ground were fantastic and every bit as exciting as flying a game hawk (falcon).

Contact on pheasant in mid-air. (Note the long legs of the Harris hawk.)

cock. For the Harris hawk, however, vastly superior in my opinion in manoeuvrability, successful flights at woodcock can be achieved.

Woodcock migrate down from the north into Scotland in late autumn. Their first sign of arrival is their nightly display by moonlight over their wood of residence. This quarry is just about impossible unless your bird will work with a good pointing dog. They do like very thick cover and are just about invisible when on the ground. Your first priority is to get a point! Once established, your bird will need to be elevated in trees as close to the point as possible.

Woodcock are very jumpy, so great care must be taken to move slowly and quietly. The trick is to get your bird to leave the tree almost simultaneously as the woodcock flushes. One way to achieve this is to throw a piece of food at the woodcock. Your bird's first reaction will be to drop on the food, but if the woodcock flushes, it will almost certainly change its attention to the flushed quarry. If it can come to terms with it before it has reached full speed and manoeuvrability, you should have some success.

17.8 The grey squirrel

Grey squirrels have a bite like a pit bull so extreme care must be taken if a painful and costly bite to your bird is to be avoided. Flights on squirrel can be amazing, but only go for these flights if you have absolutely nothing else to hunt. Flights at squirrel on the ground are seldom available or successful.

One method I have found that works is that of dray poking. Find a suitable squirrel dray in a broadleaf tree, which offers your bird an elevated stance in another tree above (steep banks on which trees grow are ideal). Take the time to get your bird into the perfect position, which

The grey squirrel has a bite like a gin trap.

can be achieved by encouraging the bird to follow you, or to try to swing your bird into this position.

Then utilise aluminium telescopic poles with which we poke at the dray. Any self-respecting resident will shoot out in search of escape. Fantastic flights can ensue with predator and prey spiralling around the tree trunk, often plunging at full speed. As your bird and the squirrel are usually heading downwards, gravity helps your bird drop to the ground with its prey, rather than settling in the fork of a branch.

Get to the scene as quickly as possible and despatch the squirrel with, say, a sharpened screwdriver through the spine, as it only takes seconds for the tables to turn, putting your bird on the receiving end of those teeth! Any bites incurred almost always go very septic. Always keep the bite area very clean, administer antibiotics and pray!

Brambles and a fox

In my job as a professional falconer, I was hunting with two American businessmen along with three Harris hawks through some scrub land. The birds were following along through woodland, when the first bird dropped like a rock from its lofty perch. It dived under a fallen tree into brambles, closely followed by the other two hawks.

Thinking we had caught a rabbit, I dived in there. I was utterly amazed to discover three very aggressive, excited Harris hawks pinning down and muzzling one large, utterly shocked fox! Two had it around the muzzle and the third on the shoulder. The fox was effectively anchored down by both brambles and birds.

My guests would not enter the heavy cover to help me; I had no knife to despatch the fox who was thrashing around, so I realised that I would have to strangle it! As I grabbed it around the neck, one of the muzzling birds changed its footing to grab me, releasing its hold on the fox. The other muzzling bird, assuming the other was abandoning ship, let go also and stepped to one side as the fox renewed its struggle with the help of snapping teeth. My sudden jump of pain (when grabbed by the first bird) obviously frightened the third bird sufficiently to jump off also, allowing the fox to get clean away, whilst I remained with one Harris hawk firmly attached to my hand and two other birds eyeing me with an expression that said, "why did you go and do that then?"

hygiene. Your bird's accommodation must be cleaned and disinfected on a daily basis, using bird/animal-safe disinfectants such as Virkon S, as directed by the manufacturer.

Special attention must be paid to food preparation or feeding surfaces as a potential point of infection, both for the sake of your bird and yourself. Preparation of your bird's food should be no different to how you would prepare your own, ensuring food is correctly thawed, surfaces and utensils disinfected prior to and after preparation.

19.1 Signs of illness

Wild birds of prey are always alert to the signs of illness or weakness in their prey. Indeed it is this ability that allows them to exploit many prey items. On the opposite side of the coin, this means that they are extremely good at masking any signs of illness in themselves, knowing only too well that they, in turn, may become a prey item to another bird of prey. Having an intimate knowledge of your bird will allow you to identify early signs of illness, allowing effective treatment before it's too late.

Some common signs that may indicate disease or injury to your bird are listed below:
- Weight loss.
- Loss of appetite.
- Unwilling to move; feathers fluffed up.
- Eyes closed; sleeping in daylight hours.
- Change in mutes or castings.
- Abnormal breathing.
- Change in voice.
- Exercise intolerance.

19.2 Loss of weight

If your bird is losing weight, it may be simply a result of your inability to balance its feeding against exercise. If your hawk was worked hard the day previously and the food not increased accordingly, or there is a sudden drop in temperature, common sense would suggest an increase in food is in order.

Husbandry: Food preparation and hygiene

It pays to get into a good routine of food preparation and hygiene. I like to defrost my food twenty-four hours before I need to use it, which I do by placing it into a fly-proof container at room temperature. It pays to defrost 40 percent more than you think you may need, just in case of emergencies. Once defrosted I place it in a refrigerator until it is needed.

There will be occasions when you will not have enough food thawed out in time and more is required in a hurry. In these circumstances I use warm water (not hot), which gently defrosts food reasonably quickly (although is does mildly affect its nutritional quality.

The use of a microwave should be avoided, as it defrosts through cooking the outer layers, allowing the radiated heat to defrost a little more into the centre. This cooking effect will compromise the hawk food and will result in mild stomach upsets in your bird.

To ensure hygiene, I clean my weathering/chamber on a daily basis, which is why it can be beneficial to have two distinct areas, allowing you the luxury of another area in which the bird can be kept whilst this goes on.

Pick up any casts and pick up any heavily soiled areas of gravel. Spray the area with a solution of Virkon S and rake over, spraying the freshly turned gravel once more. Clean and disinfect any perch areas daily.

Once a week I bring in the heavy artillery in the form of the jet wash, which, provided your accommodation drains well enough, should allow a much more thorough cleaning.

Most falconers choose not to clean as regularly during the moult, as disturbance may cause feather damage in the form of "pinched" or "fretted" feathers (see Chapter 20: The Moult).

If your chamber is designed correctly, it may be possible to integrate an area around the food station into which you can tempt your bird and then restrict by way of a sliding door or hatch.

Once restricted your bird will be oblivious to your cleaning activities, allowing you to keep its accommodation spotless.

Birds carry a range of parasites, both internal and external. An overburden of internal parasites may be another factor in a bird losing weight. An accurate diagnosis may be made by examination of the faeces, which should be done at least twice yearly by your veterinary surgeon who can prescribe the correct treatment. This is just a simple case of collecting a suitable sample on a piece of sterile plastic placed under your bird's perch, collected and transported in a sterile container to your veterinarian. From there, your veterinarian will have the sample cultured allowing a bacterial count, which will identify any imbalance. These imbalances, once identified, may be easily treated.

19.3 Loss of appetite

Any bird that is flicking food or vomiting should be presented to your veterinary surgeon as soon as possible. A bird showing these signs can deteriorate rapidly, so the "wait-and-see" approach often used for larger cats and dogs is not an option; a diagnosis needs to be formulated rapidly and treatment started.

The intestinal system of all animals is populated with a range of micro-organisms, but disease, stress, shock, dietary changes, etc., can cause an imbalance of these bacteria, resulting in diarrhoea, vomiting, loss of appetite and weight loss. This again needs to be identified rapidly through faecal culture and an appropriate antibiotic course.

A sick hawk should be handled as little as possible. However, if your bird is at flying weight, there will be little reserve of either nutrition or hydration for it to call upon. In an emergency, to buy a little time before the hawk can be presented to a veterinarian, one technique that can be utilised to prevent dehydration is the use of crop tubing. This technique is ideally learned on a healthy bird before it is needed in an emergency situation. This is a good method of hydrating or feeding a bird with poor appetite, as well as giving medication. Always remember hydrating a sick bird is more important than feeding a sick bird.

A crop tube may be made from a sterilised length—about four to six inches (10–15 cm)—of thin plastic tubing (the type that is normally used with aquariums) attached to a syringe. With an assistant holding the bird in an upright position from behind, you should take hold of the bird's head gently with one hand and open the beak by inserting a finger between the mandibles (it is less painful at the angle/back of the mouth). The tube is then inserted with the other hand, passing over the opening of the windpipe, which is seen as a slit at the back of the tongue and into the oesophagus. If done correctly, the passage of the pipe should be felt through the skin as it passes down into the crop.

Fluids sold as electrolyte powders (which are reconstituted with water) available from any veterinary practice or pharmacist are the most appropriate to hydrate. In an emergency, a tablespoon of glucose and a teaspoon of salt in one pint (.5 l) of warm water will do. These solutions should be given warm at a rate of 1 to 2 percent of the hawk's body weight, i.e., 10 to 20 ml (.3–.6 oz) for a 1 kg (2.2 lb) hawk per hour (or preferably a half dose every thirty minutes). Once administered, the hawk should still be held in the upright cast position for a few moments to ensure it does not regurgitate the con-

Checking the mute

Close examination of your hawk's mutes will highlight any potential problems of a digestive nature. The mutes consist of three distinct parts: urates (the white component), faeces (the dark, brown/black component) and water. Disease may show signs in any one part of the mutes, so regular, close examination should be conducted. Any change in the mutes may indicate disease and as such a sample should be sent to your veterinary surgeon for examination.

You may be able to identify certain parasitic conditions such as worms simply by looking a little closer at them on a daily basis. Blood or eggs will be quite apparent as will worm body sections.

A common anomaly in mutes is green staining. The green stain is bile and is often present if your bird has not been fed or is dropping in weight. This, in itself, is nothing to worry about, but if you have fed your bird a reasonable meal and the mute are still green, you may have a problem. Prolonged periods without food can be extremely detrimental to your bird's health. A fat, healthy bird would easily withstand short periods of unsuccessful hunting in the wild.

United Kingdom) and in birds that are going through some kind of physical trauma, i.e., a very jumpy tethered bird or a bird that has had heavy collisions whilst hunting.

I am convinced that this condition is caused by a number of factors. Let us assume that you are hunting on a winter's day and your bird has a few pretty hard tumbles with rabbits. During these tumbles, your bird is bound to bang the wing tips, which will become bruised slightly. On returning home, your bird is placed in its chamber or out on the weathering for the night. If the night is a cold one and the temperature drops below freezing, the bruised part of the wing starts to inflame, resulting in swelling and dry gangrene settling in as the circulation is lost in that part of the wing.

Avoiding this condition is far easier than curing it, and I have adopted a husbandry technique that has kept my birds free from this disorder for more than six years. After hunting in a cold winter's day, I do not return my hawk to either weathering or chamber, I keep it overnight in its travel box. Being a smaller airspace, the bird is able to keep warm with just its body heat. Some professional falconers I know artificially heat their chambers, which is not only expensive, but also takes your bird though a much greater temperature range in a twenty-four hour period, encouraging other medical problems to occur. By adopting the husbandry technique I have described, you stand a much greater chance of avoiding this condition.

Treatment of this condition in the initial stages involves warming and massaging the affected area. I have found a normal hair dryer invaluable for this purpose. Great care must be taken to avoid puncturing the watery cysts that form. The bird should be exercised as normal, encouraging use of the wing as well as keeping the bird's metabolic rate higher, which helps to increase circulation. Various medications have also been attempted, using vascular stimulants, such as Preparation H, corticosteroids and antibiotics, but the outcome is often poor as the end of the wing is often lost. If an application of topical ointments is unavoidable, it should be performed with care to prevent excessive oiling on the plumage. By allowing the feathers around the effected area to become greased up, you are lowering the insulation to this area. It has to be said that like so many other conditions, wing tip oedema may be avoided with attention to good husbandry.

19.9 First-aid kit

You will increase your chances of treating any condition if you can administer immediate first aid. Compile a small kit that you can carry around in your hawking bag. You'll only ever need it once for this to be a worthwhile operation. I would recommend it contain the following:

- Antiseptic spray or cream.
- Crop tube and syringe.
- Electrolyte solution.
- A/D feline diet.
- Styptic pencil.
- Small hypothermic blanket.
- Sterile dressing.
- Adhesive plaster tape.
- Small scissors.

In addition, I would recommend that you also carry a small number of sterile tubes in your mews, which can be used for mute samples or saliva swabs. The antiseptic spray and bandages are also often needed to treat the falconer.

Chapter 20

The Moult

Feathers are very complicated structures and, although amazing, do wear out quickly. For this reason they need to be changed annually. Depending on where you are in the world, Mother Nature will give your bird subtle signals to start its moult.

This is normally initiated in the spring, after an influx of young, inexperienced prey fall victim to the bird. The increased body weight and condition that this causes basically says to the bird, "You're in very good condition, there is lots of easy-to-catch food items in the area. You can afford the luxury of becoming a little slower and less manoeuvrable whilst you change your feathers."

If your bird is conditioned by appetite, i.e., at flying weight, these subtle signals don't take place and the moult will not start. You can initiate it, however, by ceasing to free fly your bird, cutting off all of its equipment and turning it loose in its chamber. Feeding your hawk as much as it will eat over this period should trigger the moult.

20.1 Moulting begins

The feathers drop in matched pairs on each side of the body and wings, allowing the bird the ability to fly, but not so efficiently. The manufacture of feathers takes place in the body at the feather follicle, where keratin (the same material as human hair and nails) is produced. The quills form, and the blood contained within them at

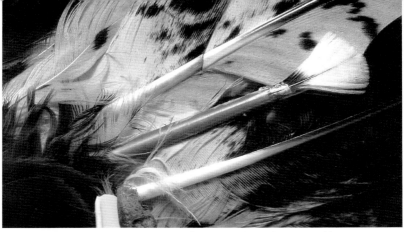
A new tail feather in blood. (Note the feather to the right is imped.)

this stage feed the feathers throughout their growth. Once the quill is fully grown, the blood retreats back up the feather and into the body. The feather then hardens and is ready to use.

When the feathers are developing, the webbing is wrapped in a wax-like sheath that the bird preens, allowing the webbing to burst out. When your bird preens it has an oil gland at the base of its tail that allows it to waterproof these new feathers against the elements. Human skin contact with the feathers removes this protective oil, which is why it is important that you do not repeatedly stroke your bird!

As the feathers contain blood, any sudden knock or bang may cause them to break or pinch. Pinched feathers may bleed for quite some time, creating a potential point of infection. The subsequent feather will cease to develop and will remain like this for a twelve-month period until the next moult. If this feather happens to be an outer primary or tail feather, this may seriously impede your bird's flight and performance.

When a new feather develops it relies in some small way on the feathers around it to guide it into position. A broken feather should ideally be repaired, even when the bird is about to moult, for this very reason.

If a bird suffers any prolonged period of hunger or has a poor-quality diet at this point, the feather production may be compromised, resulting in what we call a "fret mark," which is an obvious point of weakness in the feather. On the other hand, feeding the bird as much food as it likes will break the bond it has with the falconer, making it less co-operative and possibly even returning it to its original wild state.

A period of stress may also result in fret marks, as your bird tells its body to stop manufacturing feathers and put this energy to a more defensive use. For this reason, it is not a good idea to try to fly your bird through the moult.

The moult may take anywhere up to six months to complete, and throughout this period your bird will require a reasonably quality diet as well as minimal disturbance. You may accurately predict how far your bird has gone with its moult by looking at which feathers have been moulted.

Normally, hawks lose their tail feathers in matched pairs, going from the centre feathers out. At this point, they will start to lose primary feathers starting in the centre of the primaries, moving in to the wing and then finally moulting the outer wing primaries. Body feathers are moulted sporadically; certain larger eagles may take two moulting seasons to complete a full body, wing and tail moult.

20.2 From juvenile to mature plumage

Your Harris hawk will undergo quite a metamorphosis in this period, going from its spangled juvenile plumage to its rather splendid dark mature plumage with vivid white under-tail coverts and tail-bar, as a well as its bay wing colours. Your red-tail will obtain its trademark russet red tail and beautiful range of russet body feathers, completed by the trademark *Buteo* "bib."

The purpose of juvenile plumage is another very clever adaptation in nature. Birds of prey can be very territorial, defending the area in which they hunt and therefore protecting their food source to sustain them. Any intruders will not be looked kindly upon as they will potentially steal food, therefore becoming competitors in life. Some birds will actually kill intruders if the more subtle signals of territory defence are not hindered.

The eyass obviously needs to find and claim a territory of its own. Juvenile plumage is effectively its passport. Juvenile colouration is an obvious sign of youth and therefore inexperience. Mother Nature tells the older, more experienced residential birds that the interlopers are young and inexperienced, and therefore not such a great threat. If they gently harass them, they'll move on their way, resulting in a natural, geographic distribution of the species.

Another feature of juvenile feathers is that the wing and tail feathers are often longer than their adult feathers. This offers the young bird greater balance like the trainer wheels of a bike, but less speed as they create drag. The mature feathers are shorter, making them faster at a time when they are more experienced flyers. Nature is truly an amazing thing.

20.3 Moult complete

Once the moult is complete, you can start to think about the retraining of your bird. Before you think about re-catching and equipping your hawk, you may want to reduce its food intake for a couple of days, which will save time in the retraining process.

The retraining process will very much shadow your original training process, the only difference will be that the whole process will only take fractionally as long. Your bird's weight may have to be reduced slightly lower than it was when you finished flying it in the previous season, but an overall increase in body weight should be the eventual result in the second season.

20.4 Repairing feathers

Broken feathers are the result of bad management or housing, and are the mark of a poor falconer. Pride yourself on the condition of your bird's feathers and endeavour to keep them looking as smart and as beautiful as seen in its wild counterpart.

Feathers do get bent, however, and if left will result in breakage,

A bent (not broken) feather will, when heated in water, return to its original shape.

leading to more feather damage. The tail and wing feathers are like a pack of fanned playing cards, if one is suddenly removed, its neighbours lose support and topple.

If a feather is not repaired as soon as it is broken, the feathers around it will soon follow suit. The quill of a developed feather contains a vacuum of air; if bent, the action of heating the air, either by hot air or water, will expend this air within the vacuum and straighten it to its original shape.

If you watch wildlife programs about Africa, you will see soaring birds like vultures sitting in the early morning sun with wings outstretched. Because they spend so much time on the wing soaring, their primary feathers get bent upwards. These early morning sessions allow the sun to straighten their feathers back into their original shape.

Provided the feather is bent and not broken, the vacuum will be intact and dipping can be performed. Get a container of boiling water deep enough to take the feather in question. Cast the bird and dip the feather into the boiling water. This will straighten it in seconds, but be careful that the bird does not get loose or get scalded! Dipping may make feathers brittle, so try to avoid doing it too much.

If the quill is broken, dipping will not work; air bubbles will be visible in the hot water from the breakage site. Your only option is to "imp" (repair) the feather. Primary feathers are incredibly hard to imp successfully, and bridging is an option you may want to try. To bridge, take an old similar feather and remove the webbing from the sides.

Next, split the feather down the centre using a sharp scalpel, leaving you with a top and bottom section. Select a section approximately three-quarters-of-an-inch (2-cm) long and of the same approximate diameter as that of the breakage area. Glue these sections using superglue, first the top and then the bottom of the broken feather.

This may not be as cosmetically nice as an imp, but it will offer the broken feather support and should last to the end of the season.

Broken tail feathers can be imped properly, and if done correctly this repair will be invisible. Find an old tail feather that matches the position and angle of the broken feather perfectly. Hood and cast the bird in a soft cloth or towel and place, breast down with its feet pressing into a cushion or towel.

Take a piece of card and slip it up and around the tail feathers, isolating the broken one, and then wrap the card around the rest of the tail, clipping it into position with small bulldog clips.

A broken feather is cut, a donor half is found, and a suitable imping needle is made from carbon fibre. / The imp needle is inserted in the centre of the feather quills.

Finally, a small drop of Super Glue is placed at the joint area, leaving an almost invisible mend.

If the breakage is near the base of the tail, the thickness of the feather will make it almost impossible to imp so you will need to cut the feather at a diagonal about three-quarters of an inch (2 cm) from its root (avoid cutting the webbing).

Position the donor feather against the tail and match it up for length, cutting it in a corresponding position and angle. The angle will allow the feather to lock correctly and stop it from spinning. Next take a piece of a carbon-fibre fishing rod tip and cut a piece around about three-quarters-of-an-inch (2-cm) long. Split it with your scalpel to make a diameter, which will just squeeze into the feather quill. Make a point on both ends and slide one half into the donor feather, then try it for size, sliding the other half into your bird's feather.

The material used for the imping needle is very important. I like carbon fibre as pieces of this size and diameter mimic the bend and flex of your bird's tail feather. Old books talk of needles being made of rusted iron pins, but I would doubt their effectiveness over a period of time.

If completely happy with the fit and match of the needle, pull the two halves apart slightly and apply your glue to the areas around the join. Quickly slide both halves back together, holding the bird still whilst it cures or dries.

Finally, sprinkle a little flour around the area of gluing to absorb any stray glue, before removing the card and taking your bird back onto the fist.

Don't do as a friend of mine once did and superglue yourself to your bird. You'll look very strange at the hospital emergency ward!

20.5 Coping

In the wild, a bird's beak will never need to be trimmed. It will be kept to the right length and shape by constant wear on large bones and the like.

In captivity, no matter how careful you are, you will eventually have to "cope" (trim) an overgrown beak. An overgrown beak will, if left uncorrected, present a variety of problems. The area along the top mandible will crack or break if your bird bites on something hard, resulting in a large crack. Meat will stick in this crack and the subsistent bacteria will increase its size. If left unattended the beak may actually shear off or become infected.

Trimming, or coping, a beak may seem a little daunting if you have never done it before, but having the right tools and files on hand will simplify the procedure greatly. You will need the following:

- A chainsaw file.
- A selection of smaller files.
- Snips or side cutters.
- Fine sandpaper.
- A styptic pencil.

As we have dealt with Harris hawks throughout this book, I shall describe the coping of a Harris. The only difference between trimming the beak of this species and a falcon is you need to recreate the falcon's "tooth" on the upper mandible when trimming.

Hood and cast your bird in a soft cloth or towel, holding it in an upright position. You will probably have to remove the hood in order to perform this operation, but before you do, take a good look at the beak and decide exactly how much it needs to be trimmed and where. You may like to use the point of one of your smaller files to etch your intended file mark on either side of the beak.

Remove the hood and start cutting off the overgrown point of the beak using your snips or side cutters. The beak contains a blood-carrying quick, which runs centrally. If the beak is very overgrown or you cut the beak too short, it may bleed. Use your styptic pencil to stop the flow of blood by pressing on until the flow is stemmed.

Next, take off the excess beak material using your chainsaw file. Place a finger into the corner of your bird's mouth, encouraging it to open its beak. Keep your finger in this position being careful not to catch the soft upper and lower mouth tissue with your file. This may be achieved by angling your file at forty-five degrees to the beak surface.

This beak is overgrown, which will eventually lead to cracking. / The tip of the beak is removed to the desired length

A finger is placed in the mouth, both to hold the beak still and to protect the tongue. / Using the chain saw file, cope any excessive beak material around the upper mandible sides, upper mandible tip and lower mandible.

The beak is returned to an acceptable length.

Reshape the beak and finely file any areas using your smaller coping files. The lower mandible should also be taken down a little, but again be very careful of the soft inner mouth tissue and tongue.

Finally, use your fine sandpaper to gently rub any sharp edges left on the outside of the beak.

Re-hood your bird and stand it back on your fist. Allow it a couple of minutes to settle down and then remove the hood and give it a small food reward. By doing this you will encourage your bird to salivate, removing particles from its mouth, as well as rebuild the bond you may have broken by such behaviour.

Chapter 21

Looking to the Future

With the help of this book and a modicum of common sense, you should now have a bird that is hunting in various styles and has a variety of quarry under its belt, but more importantly you will have a great understanding of how you achieved this. You may have made some mistakes, but everybody's human, and as long as you realise where you went wrong, your future in falconry is bright.

21.1 Learning has just begun

At this stage, most falconers start to drift over to what I comically term as the "Dark Side," thinking that they have learned all there is to know. In reality, you will never stop learning, and you have the best teacher in the world if you know how to listen to your hawk!

Many young Austringers (trainer of hawks) think that the challenge is over once they have trained their Harris hawk and try to move on to other species like goshawks and sparrow hawks. I feel that this is their biggest mistake. Fly your Harris every season. Imagine the flights that you would like to achieve and the ways in which you feel your Harris could be trained to achieve them, and then work towards those goals. Your Harris is smart and adaptable, and with work and time anything can be achieved. Harris hawks, of all of the species of birds I have trained, get better and better with age. Every year they will display a new behaviour or hunting strategy learned from the year before. Each season you'll marvel at just how good they are getting.

I have one Harris here in my collection, which I trained more than fifteen years ago. At eighteen years old, she is absolutely deadly in the hunting field. Her game record for last year recorded 351 kills of all types and species to her credit. She is a credit to our sport and to her species.

Here in the United Kingdom, the price of captive-bred birds has dropped dramatically over the past ten years and with this, I firmly believe, so have the standards of the sport. Rather than sticking with one bird, using patience and common sense to try to achieve results, people just go out and buy another bird, feeling that this one will be better. What happens to all of these cast-off birds? Where do they go? I know of one particular guy who has a full-time job and tries to fly twelve birds on a daily basis. He has twelve very poorly conditioned, unfit and non-motivated birds in his care.

During the moulting period of your falconry year, you may also be tempted to get a partner for your bird in an attempt to breed them. If so, read, study and prepare. There are some excellent books out there that deal with captive breeding and incubation. If you have the time and attention span, this can be a great achievement. Your hawk will have a pastime and a focus throughout the summer period, and make its life in captivity more worthwhile. But try to only breed the number of young that you know you can find good homes for.

There is no money in captive breeding. Ask any of the larger breeders! It may, however, teach you more about your chosen species of hunting bird. I, after so many years in the sport, am still learning, discovering and enjoying.

21.2 Protecting the future of falconry

Falconry for me is not only my hobby or my job; it is my way of life. I owe everything I have, my home, my wife and my family, to this sport, and do not want irresponsible beginners and poor wildlife legislation here in the United Kingdom to bring it into disrepute.

In the United States, falconers are developing new styles of flight, husbandry techniques and breeding techniques, all of which are fully backed by federal and state government. Having access to vast expanses of open ground on which to hunt, they are able to fully appreciate and develop the birds in their care and the simulations of their wild counterparts. For U.S. falconers, the future looks pretty good!

However, over the next ten years here in the United Kingdom, the countryside, its workforce and its inhabitants are going to realise traumatic change. For economic reasons, the wealthy landowners providing both employment and accommodation are becoming a thing of the past, being replaced by faceless corporate owners of estates, forestry and vast tracts of land. These new owners often have no concerns for the game and wildlife on this ground.

The humble dwellings of the common rural people are becoming fashionable barn conversions, the "des-res" of well-to-do businesspeople, who have very little understanding of rural industry or affairs. It's becoming difficult for the country person to afford to live here anymore. Representative government bodies are making life-shattering decisions about country life, many of whom are driven by electoral promises to financiers. The anti-hunt brigade is finally getting its way. Every falconer, huntsman and game shot is under the spotlight of the politically correct town dweller. You cannot fight the inexorable tide. Money and majority talk.

As a result, the future of falconry in the United Kingdom is looking grim, unless we practise and promote our sport to the highest possible standard! We have a responsibility to our forefathers, the founders of this marvellous sport, that it does not die out in our lifetime. So what can you do?

First, strive for excellence in everything you do. Fly your bird daily to a high standard, keeping equipment and accommodation clean and presentable. Learn as much as you can about not only the techniques used in this sport, but also the sport's history. Learn as much as you can about the birds in your charge, their Latin name, their distribution and habits in the wild. Keep only those birds to which you can offer daily exercise and care. You are now a representative of the sport. It is your responsibility to represent us well. Be intolerant of the falconers who do not keep their birds or accommodation well. Suggest, teach and help if possible to drive our standards higher.

Also, look the part. Don't go out in jeans and Kammo jacket.

Wear clothing that is suitable to your hobby's elevated station. How many driven game shots go out in Kammo gear? I am appalled at the standard of some so-called professional falconers—their birds, broken-feathered dejected creatures, sitting on mute-strewn blocks with tatty equipment.

It is not enough just to have a bird fly, even if it is spectacular in the hunting field. It must mimic its wild counterpart in performance as well as appearance if we are to stand a chance of keeping this sport alive! Bad husbandry will get this sport banned. Discourage or publicly denounce anyone who you know does not practise your sport to such high standards. Your fellow falconer is your future. Stand together, proud in the fact that you are one of just a few dedicated enough to practise this sport to such a high standard, and carry it into the next millennium.

Further Reading

Books on Falconry

Beebe, Frank. 1984. *A Falconry Manual.* BC: Hancock House Publishers.

Beebe, Frank. 1992. *The Compleat Falconer.* BC: Hancock House Publishers.

Ford, Emma. 1998. *Falconry: Art and Practice.* (revised edition). New York: Sterling Publishing.

Chancellor, Meyburg. 2000. *Raptors at Risk.* BC: Hancock House Publishers.

Dekker, Dick, Court, Gordon. 1999. *Bolt from the Blue.* BC: Hancock House Publishers.

Fox, Nick. 1995. *Understanding the Bird of Prey.* BC: Hancock House Publishers.

Glasier, Philip. 1963. *As the Falcon Her Bells.* UK: Heinemann.

Glasier, Philip. 1978. *Falconry and Hawking.* UK: Batsford.

Haak, Bruce. 1992. *Hunting Falcon.* BC: Hancock House Publishers.

Haak, Bruce. 1995. *Pirate of the Plains.* BC: Hancock House Publishers.

Hollinshead, Martin. 1993. *Hawking Ground Quarry.* BC: Hancock House Publishers.

Mavrogordato, Jack. 1960. *A Hawk for the Bush: A treatise on the training of the sparrow-hawk and other short-winged hawks.* UK: F. & G. Witherby.

O'Brien, Dan. 1997. *The Rites of Autumn: A Falconer's Journey Across the American West.* UK: The Lyons Press.

Oakes, W.C. 1994. *The Falconer's Apprentice: A Guide to Training the Passage Red-Tailed Hawk.* US: Eagle Wing Publishing.

Upton, Roger. 2002. *Arab Falconry.* BC: Hancock House Publishers.

Upton, Roger. 1989. *O' For a Falconer's Voice: Memories of the Old Hawking Club.* UK: Crowood Press.

Books on Dog Training

Oakes, W.C., et al. *Rabbit Hawker's Dogs.* US: Eagle Wing Publishing.

Wallace, Guy. 2002. *The Specialist Gundog.* UK: Sportsman's Press.

Wallace, Guy. 1995. *The Versatile Gundog: Training H.P.R's for Gun, Rifle and Hawk.* UK: Sportsman's Press.

Books on Raptor Health and First Aid

Cooper, John E., Cooper, Margaret. 2003. *Captive Birds in Health and Disease.* BC: Hancock House Publishers.

Forbes, Neil. A. *Field First Aid for Birds of Prey.* Campaign for Falconry.

Forbes, Neil. A. and Flint, Colin. G. 2000. *Raptor Nutrition. UK:* Honeybrook Animal Foods.

Naisbitt, Richard, Holz, Peter. 2004. *Captive Raptor Management & Rehabilitation.* BC: Hancock House Publishers.

Redig, P.T., et al. 1993. *Raptor Biomedicine.* US: University of Minnesota Press.

Contacts of Interest

Equipment Suppliers

Ben Long Falconry Equipment
P.O. Box 164
Exeter
EX4 7WB
UK
Tel: 01392 257424
Fax: 01392 460173
E-mail: benlongfalconry@aol.com
Web site: www.benlongfalconry.com

Deben Ferret Finders and Ferret Products
Deben Group Industries Ltd.
Deben Way, Melton, Woodbridge
Suffolk
IP12 1RS
Tel: 0870 4422600
Fax: 0870 4430110
Web site: www.deben.com

Martin Jones Falconry Furniture
(hood specialists)
The Parsonage
Llanrothal, Monmouth
NP5 3QJ
UK
Tel: 01600 750300
Fax: 01600 750450

Northwood's Limited
P.O. Box 874
Rainer, WA 98576
U.S.A.
Tel: (+1) 360 446 3212
Fax: (+1) 360 446 1270
E-mail: northwoods@olywa.net

The Author's Falconry School

Phoenix Falconry Ltd.
Gardeners Cottage
Braco Castle Estate
Braco, Perthshire
FK15 9LA
Scotland
Tel: 01786 880539
Fax: 01786 880625
E-mail: scottish.falconry@virgin.net
Web site:www.scottishfalconry.co.uk

Government Bodies

Canadian Wildlife Service
Web site: www.cws-scf.ec.gc.ca

Department for Environment, Food and Rural Affairs (DEFRA)
Nobel House
17 Smith Square
London, UK
SW1P 3JR
Tel: 020 7238 6000
Fax: 020 7238 6591

U.S. Fisheries and Wildlife Service
E-mail: contact@fws.gov
Web site: www.fws.gov

List of Major Falconry Magazines & Clubs

American Falconry Magazine
725 Smith Street
Dayton, WY USA 82836-0187
Web site: www.americanfalconry.com/

British Falconer's Club
Web site:
www.britishfalconersclub.co.uk/

The British Hawking Association
Web site: www.thebha.co.uk/contact.htm

California Hawking Club
Web site: www.calhawkingclub.org

The Hawk Board
Web site: www.hawkboard.org.uk

The Falconers & Raptor Conservation Magazine
PO Box 464,
Berkhamsted, Herts HP4 2UR
England
Web site: www.falconclubs.fsnet.co.uk/
falconersmagazine.htm

International Falconer Magazine
Turkey Court, Ashford Road,
Maidstone, KEN ME14 5PP
England
Web site: www.intfalconer.com/

Irish Hawking Journal
Web site: www.irishhawkingclub.com

Italian Falconry Club
Web site: http://web.tiscali.it/yarak/

North American Falconers Association Journal
Web site: www.n-a-f-a.org/

Scottish Hawking Club
Crookedstane,
Elvanfoot, By Biggar
Lanarkshire ML12 6RL
UK

Tinnunculus, Deutscher Falkenorden
Web site: www.falkenorden.de/
bayern/infos/

The Welsh Hawking Club
Web site: www.thewelshhawking
club.com

Hancock House Publishers
The World Publisher for Raptor and Falconry Titles

See a full listing of our titles:
Web site: www.hancockhouse.com

PHOTOS WANTED
Good photos are always wanted for upcoming books. We generally do not pay for photos but will give credit on book purchases. We always give credits and, if you wish, your address. All raptor and other bird species needed.

Glossary

Aspergilosis: Dangerous fungus that can affect a bird's respiratory system.

Austringer: Trainer of hawks.

Bating: Jump from the fist or perch in an attempt to get away.

Bewitt: A piece of leather on the leg to secure bells or telemetry.

Block: An individual perch to which the hawk is tethered.

Bowsing: When birds throw their heads back violently to get fluid into their throats.

Bumblefoot: Foot infection causing swelling.

Carriage: Training time when you carry your bird around.

Cast: A pair of birds.

Casting: A torpedo-shaped object birds cough up after a meal has been processed.

Cere: The soft area of skin above its beak.

Cope: Trim beak or claws.

Creance: A long string wrapped around a stick used in training.

Crop: A storage bag next to the throat where food can be placed.

Entering: Flying at quarry for the first time.

Eyass: A bird that has never experienced wild flight.

Fledging: Leaving the nest.

Following on: Teaching a bird to fly by following.

Free lofting: Setting a bird loose.

Frounce: A canker of the throat and mouth.

Gauntlet: A glove.

Group: A number of birds flying together but not co-operatively.

Haggard: A bird taken from the wild in mature plumage.

High jumping: A series of vertical jumps to your fist, in quick succession.

Hood: Leather cap to blindfold a hawk.

Imping: Repairing a broken feather.

Imprinted: A bird's belief that humans are their parents or food providers.

Jess: Strap attached to legs of a trained hawk.

Lamping: Catching rabbits at night.

Making in: Approaching a bird.

Manning: Humanisation.

Mantling: Stretching out wings over a kill or food.

Mews: Name for the building in which a falcon or hawk is housed.

Moult: Change of feathers.

Mutes: Droppings.

Pack: A group of birds that hunts co-operatively.

Passage: A bird taken from the wild in juvenile plumage.

Slips: The quarry at which you release a bird.

Swivel: Used in the leash so that the hawk cannot get twisted.

Telemetry: Tracking devices.

Thermalling: Using pockets of warm air to gain height.

Tirings: Tougher pieces of food.

Index